Pocket Guide to Crime Scene Photography

Pocket Guide to Crime Scene Photography

Mark E. Vecellio
Erick P. Bryant

CRC Press is an imprint of the
Taylor & Francis Group, an **informa** business

CRC Press
Taylor & Francis Group
6000 Broken Sound Parkway NW, Suite 300
Boca Raton, FL 33487-2742

First issued in paperback 2021

ISBN-13: 978-0-367-78755-4 (pbk)
ISBN-13: 978-1-4987-6823-8 (hbk)

Visit the Taylor & Francis Web site at
http://www.taylorandfrancis.com

and the CRC Press Web site at
http://www.crcpress.com

Contents

Preface

There are many outstanding forensic photography textbooks currently available; ones that provide excellent insight and advanced knowledge of a wide range of techniques and theory. This book is not intended to compete with those, but instead offer a basic, yet accurate, guide to crime scene photography. For those who find the technical terms and jargon associated with photography and digital imaging to be complicated, then this book is for you!

Not every CSI, investigator, or patrol officer has the time, nor the interest, in becoming an expert photographer. But from our years of experience, we know that, as a professional community, we care deeply about performing our duties. This handbook will allow you to improve your proficiency while maximizing your time investment.

You will be provided the know-how, step-by-step, to properly document a crime scene through use of photography. Much of the methodology presented will apply to virtually any crime scene, but in addition, specialized instructions are provided for scenes or evidence which pose difficulty or require unique methods. So not only will you have a simple, yet concise, checklist for photographing most crime scenes, but you'll also have access to step-by-step comprehensive guides to photographing evidence such as tire tracks, dust impressions, fingerprints, and luminescence from trace blood search reagents.

About the Authors

Mark E. Vecellio is currently an assistant professor of Applied Forensic Sciences at Methodist University and an adjunct instructor of Forensic Science at Fayetteville Technical Community College, in Fayetteville, North Carolina, and has previously taught as a senior instructor at the U.S. Army Military Police School and Fayetteville Technical Community College and served as adjunct faculty at both Central Texas College and Virginia College. He holds a BS in liberal studies from Excelsior College, a master's degree in public administration from the City University of Seattle, and a master's degree in forensic science from George Washington University. Mr. Vecellio has previously served in the U.S. Army Criminal Investigation Command (CID) as a special agent, supervisory special agent, and forensic sciences officer. He is a current member of numerous forensic science associations and has led investigative task forces in robbery, rape, and arson crimes.

Erick P. Bryant currently serves as a crime scene analyst with the Colorado Bureau of Investigation. He previously served with the U.S. Army CID, where he retired as the chief of the policy branch at the U.S. Army CID headquarters in Quantico, Virginia. He holds a BS in political science from Georgia Southern University and a master's degree in forensic science from George Washington University. He has expertise in the following forensic and investigative disciplines: crime scene investigation, analysis and reconstruction, forensic photography, bloodstain pattern analysis, criminal investigation, death investigation, sexual assault investigation, child abuse investigation, and interviews and interrogations. He has also served as adjunct faculty at several colleges and universities. He is a member of the American Academy of Forensic Science, the International Association of Identification (IAI), the Rocky Mountain Division of the IAI, and the Rocky Mountain Association of Bloodstain Pattern Analysts. He is certified with the IAI in both crime scene analysis and bloodstain pattern analysis.

CHAPTER 1

Providing Context

We have all heard the adage "a picture is worth a thousand words." Although most of us are unfamiliar with its origin (early twentieth-century journalism), nearly everyone comprehends the meaning: that a photograph is able to offer a visual description of a scene or object that would be very difficult to articulate through words or, for the law enforcement officer, in formal report writing. Furthermore, an advantage of photographs is the inherent objectivity—the viewer can actually see what the officer saw—especially when juxtaposed with subjective narrative accounts that are prone to experience, writing ability, bias, or simply differing analytical approaches. We are quite confident that if 100 different officers were to describe the same crime scene, we would see 100 different written accounts. So with that in mind, one can see how the use of photographs, if taken properly, can help mitigate the subjective aspects of crime scene processing and analysis.

For the official tasked with documenting crime scenes, another advantage of photography is efficiency; it is simply much quicker and less arduous to expose photographs of certain objects than to offer fully detailed descriptions. Given the current climate of budgetary restraint, logic dictates that any method which facilitates efficiency be considered.

Photographs provide records of the scene in its unaltered state, prior to evidence being moved, marked for identification, or collected. This provides immense benefits for investigators, who often refer back to crime scene photographs to search for investigative leads; assess the credibility of victims, suspects, or witnesses; or reconstruct the crime scene for analytical purposes.

A final purpose of crime scene photography is the ability to support judicial processes. An officer, through photographs, may be able to provide visual accounts of the crime scene to judges and juries. Photographs can serve as convincing evidence in the courtroom, again, possibly offsetting any potential arguments of investigator bias. By following the methods and protocols recommended in this guide, you can be assured that you did everything possible to ensure the admissibility of your photographic documentation of the scene. Figures 1.1 through 1.4 are crime scene photographs that were used to supplement other crime scene documentation.

Photographing the Scene within a Crime Scene Processing Framework

Generally speaking, photographs are one of the primary methods of documenting crime scenes, along with sketches and notes. Within some jurisdictions, three-dimensional scanning and videography is often used to supplement the basic documentation methods, especially in cases with significant interest. However,

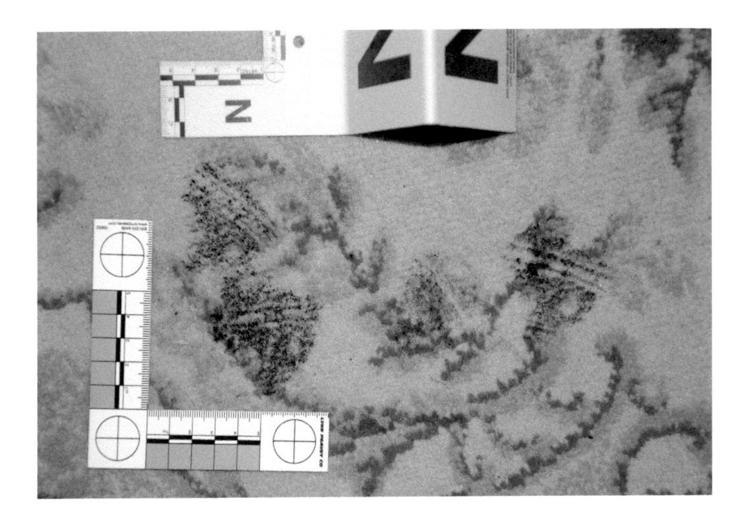

FIGURE 1.1 This image depicts a bloody footprint on a carpet that was enhanced with leucocrystal violet.

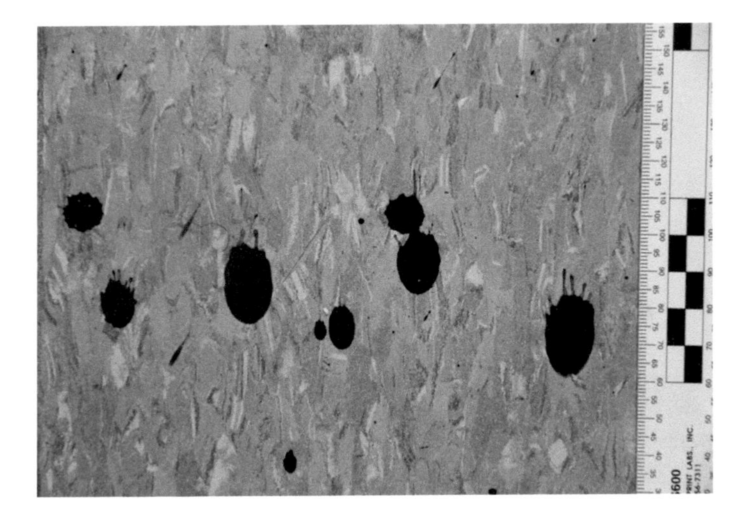

FIGURE 1.2 This image depicts a drip bloodstain pattern from a homicide investigation. Close-up images allow viewers to examine details of the evidence. For instance, with training, an investigation could determine the directionality of these bloodstains based on the images.

FIGURE 1.3 This image depicts a bloody footprint from a homicide investigation. Close-up images allow the viewer to examine fine details of the evidence. In some cases, if the images are properly taken, forensic scientists can use the images for comparison purposes.

it should be noted that even when videography and/or scanning technologies are used, photography should never be omitted.

We have found that despite the utility of the other methods, viewing photographs is often more effective, and efficient, for performing an in-depth analysis of certain crime scene details. This is not to suggest foregoing the other methods; each has its purpose and may serve to be instrumental in properly analyzing the scene or presenting findings to a jury.

As mentioned previously, crime scenes should be photographed prior to any processes that alter the scene, including placing placards and moving or collecting evidence. A simple guideline to follow is that nothing should be moved, touched, or otherwise disturbed before it is photographed, with two primary exceptions.

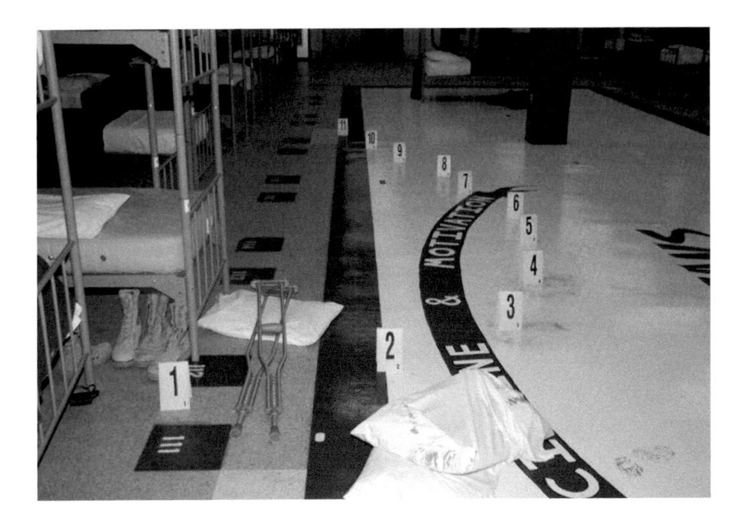

FIGURE 1.4 This image depicts bloody footwear prints. The placards were used to draw attention to the positions of the footwear prints, thus revealing the path the suspect traveled after committing the crime. Crime scene images are used to supplement notes and sketches and may be a powerful method of displaying what you, the investigator, observed at the crime scene. If taken properly, the images will accurately represent the crime scene.

The first exception to this photograph-first rule primarily involves first responders, who may be responsible for lifesaving measures. Of course, saving a life takes precedence over all other actions. The second exception, in some circumstances, might be the rapid recovery of fragile evidence that is at risk of being destroyed. One example might be a shoe impression that is in danger of being destroyed because of rain. In these cases with fragile evidence, the officer is charged with assessing whether he or she has the time to take a quick photograph or two before protecting the fragile evidence. This will ultimately be a judgment call within his or her discretion.

Finally, as with any forensic endeavor, it is always a good idea to be familiar with governing organizations and with what is considered as best practice within a particular discipline. The Scientific Working Group Imaging Technology (SWGIT.org) was such an organization. While it no longer publishes policy, its prior policies are still available online and represent what is still considered best practice within the field of forensic/crime scene photography. We recommend that crime scene photographers be familiar with this organization and its policies. In addition, there are numerous texts on the topic of forensic photography. We point out a few of these later in this book. Again, we recommend that crime scene photographers be familiar with these texts.

Chapter 2

Equipment and Accessories

The following list of camera equipment and accessories will provide the novice- or intermediate-level photographer with sufficient flexibility to allow effective photography of any crime scene or item of evidence. Keep in mind that this is not an all-inclusive list of available supplies and equipment that could be used in advanced photographic techniques. This list, however, contains the essentials and serves as an excellent starting point. Once you gain experience and if you choose to seek advanced technical knowledge, you may choose to expand upon this list. If so, we recommend *Advanced Crime Scene Photography*, second edition, by Christopher D. Duncan. This text is an excellent reference for advanced photography techniques and methods.

Prior to purchasing the following items, you can consider purchasing forensic photography packages available through some forensic retailers. These packages are often comprehensive and provide everything you will need.

- Digital single-lens reflex (DSLR) camera: Several excellent cameras are available; common brands include Nikon, Canon, and Fuji. If your agency does not use a DSLR camera and cannot purchase one, try to use a higher-end point-and-shoot model which allows control over f-stops and shutter speeds, at a minimum. We do, however, highly recommend a DSLR camera. You will have trouble obtaining certain, specialized photographs without one (Figure 2.1 is a Nikon DSLR camera).
- Lenses
  - Zoom lens: A zoom lens will allow you to zoom in or out at the scene, changing the focal length of your lens. This will afford you a great deal of flexibility. Make sure your zoom lens has wide-angle capabilities; you will want to make sure the lower number of the zoom range is below 30. This will help

FIGURE 2.1 Nikon DSLR camera with an affixed detachable flash unit.

you photograph small areas, by providing a wider perspective.

- Close-up lens: As its name implies, a close-up lens will be essential for close-up photography. You will often need to position your camera as close as you can to small items of evidence in order to capture key details. This will be possible only through the use of a close-up lens. Close-up lenses may be referred to as macro lenses or micro lenses depending on the manufacturer (Figures 2.2 and 2.3 are suitable lenses for crime scene photography).

- Flash unit: A detachable flash unit is a must to ensure sufficient light coverage. Rotating flash heads are also very useful and highly recommended. When purchasing a flash unit, keep in

FIGURE 2.2 Example of a zoom lens which allows you to zoom in or out. This type of lens would be useful for most of your crime scene photography work.

FIGURE 2.3 Example of a close-up lens which is specifically designed for close-up photography.

mind that the higher the guide number, the more powerful the flash. So higher guide numbers will provide a larger coverage area. We advise against using flash units with guide numbers below 80; they are not sufficiently powerful to provide adequate lighting for outdoor scenes.

- Ring flash: Ring flash units are very helpful for close-up work; they serve to help reduce hot-spots and evenly distribute the light.
- Flash cable: A cable that is four to six feet long is preferred, especially for photographing footwear and tire impressions. Keep in mind that most sold are in the three-foot range. We recommend checking with forensic supply distributors.
- Camera battery: We recommend always having a few extra batteries for each camera you have. When you purchase your camera, many come

with batteries. When ordering extra, make sure the batteries are compatible with your camera.

- Battery charger: When purchasing, you will need to ensure that your charger is compatible with your batteries.
- Tripod: We recommend purchasing a heavy-duty model of tripod. Quadrapods (four legs) are also available. Some tripods allow the camera to be positioned upside down which is beneficial for various forms of close-up work. We also recommend tripods that have built-in levels, which will help you ensure that your camera is positioned on a 90° plane with your evidence. This is very important for examination-quality photographs, such as footwear impressions, tire track impressions, and fingerprints.
- Remote shutter release: Some cameras require a cable while others are wireless. These are very helpful when using a tripod; you will be able to free up a hand to help hold scales, flashlights, or flash units. Remote shutter releases also help avoid camera blur on very long exposures that can be caused by depressing the shutter button on the camera (Figure 2.4 depicts two types of remote shutter releases).
- Scales: We recommend having a variety of sizes and shapes of scales available. American Board of Forensic Odontology (ABFO) scales, in an L shape, are especially useful. Some scales have built-in gray scales which can help correct color accuracy if the initial photographs displayed incorrect color shades (Figure 2.5 depicts several types of scales commonly used by crime scene photographers, including the L-shaped ABFO scale).

FIGURE 2.4 Remote shutter releases; one is a cable and one is wireless. Either type is effective.

- Filters: You may find several types of filters to be useful.
  - Polarizer: A polarizer filter reduces glare and is especially useful when photographing through glass. This filter can also help protect the lens from scratches.

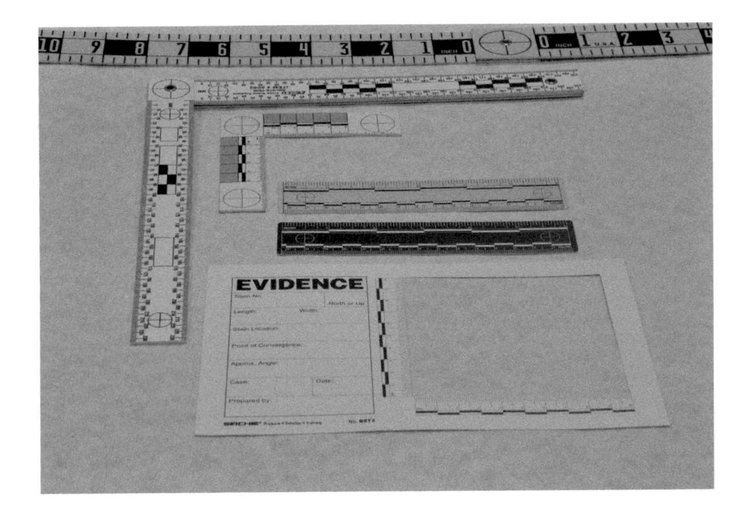

FIGURE 2.5 Examples of scales which will be used in close-up work.

  - Colored filters: Colored filters are used to block out certain types of light and are useful when photographing items that fluoresce under the power of alternate light sources. We recommend purchasing orange, red, and yellow filters. Make sure that the filters fit your camera lens; they come in different sizes.
- Camera bag: The ideal camera bag will be sturdy with sufficient padding to provide an adequate level of protection for your camera and accessories. Large bags are available that will hold just about all your accessories (Figures 2.6 and 2.7 depict common camera bags that offer protection and handy storage for the camera and accessories).
- Memory card: It is very useful to have several memory cards, particularly if you are likely to

FIGURE 2.6 A camera bag is convenient and can provide protection for your camera equipment.

FIGURE 2.7 Inside of a camera bag. This particular bag has padded partitions which provide additional protection for your equipment.

process more than one or two scenes on a single shift.

- Memory card reader and/or universal serial bus cable
- Software: Many camera manufacturers have their own software. You also might consider Adobe Photoshop once you gain experience and knowledge. Ensure to receive qualified training before enhancing images; specific procedures must be followed to ensure admissibility.
- Flashlight
- Placards: These are used to help visualize and bring attention to individual items of evidence within a crime scene (Figure 2.8).

FIGURE 2.8 Evidence placards.

危機

CHAPTER 3

Camera Terms and Photography Principles Made Easy to Understand

Camera Shooting/Exposure Modes

DSLR cameras, as well as some lesser expensive non-single-lens reflex cameras, provide photographers with a variety of shooting modes, also called exposure modes. These shooting modes allow the photographer different levels of control over the camera functions that control exposure. With practice and experience, a photographer can optimize efficiency and effectiveness through proper selection and utilization of these shooting modes. Throughout this chapter, we refer to the use of different shooting modes; this section provides a general understanding of the modes as well as some of the key advantages of each.

DSLR cameras generally have the following modes: manual (depicted as *M* on cameras), aperture priority (depicted as *A* or *AV* on cameras), shutter priority (depicted as *S* or *TV* on cameras), and fully automatic (depicted as *auto* or *program* on cameras).

In addition, many cameras have additional modes which automatically generate settings for various types of photographs, such as portraits, landscapes, movement, and close-ups. Although we do not necessarily advise against the use of these additional and various modes, we feel that focusing on the basic modes available with just about any DSLR camera will afford the photographer the necessary skill to capture any crime scene image. We generally advise against the use of the fully automatic mode unless you simply cannot operate the camera otherwise. The fully automatic mode results in a poor depth of field, thus making large portions of your photograph appear blurry. Depth of field, and methods to maximize it, is further described in the "Depth of Field" section.

The *manual* shooting mode which allows the photographer to control all camera settings, is the most versatile shooting mode and can be used to properly photograph any scene or item of evidence. Using manual mode will allow you to fine-tune shutter speeds and f-stops in order to maximize the key elements of your photograph, including exposure, depth of field, and blur prevention. Manual mode requires some technical proficiency, especially regarding the adjustment of shutter speeds and f-stops, but the benefits derived from its use are certainly worthwhile of any time and effort expended to become familiar with camera settings.

The *aperture priority* mode allows the photographer to select the f-stop, while the camera automatically selects a shutter speed to ensure a proper exposure. We believe that you will find aperture priority to be very effective in situations in which plenty of ambient light is available, or when using flash. You can select an f-stop number to achieve a sufficient depth of field and allow the camera to do the rest. Of course, if the light is dim, this will be problematic as the camera will select a slow shutter speed resulting in a blur from camera shake.

The *shutter priority* mode allows the photographer to select the shutter speed while the camera automatically selects an f-stop to achieve a proper exposure. This approach allows the photographer to obtain a properly exposed photograph while maximizing the depth of field when working in a low-light environment with no ability to add light as with a flash. Of course, shutter priority will not be effective when you wish to use a very specific f-stop.

Other Modes

Additional modes may or may not be available on your camera, depending on the manufacturer and model. The following is a brief description of some of the more common ones; you may find that if you operate a point-and-shoot camera, these modes, in addition to fully automatic, are your only choices. If you own a DSLR, we suggest foregoing the use of these modes and sticking to the three aforementioned modes: manual, aperture priority, or shutter priority.

- *Landscape:* The landscape mode is used for photographing large scenes. The camera will select a small aperture to maximize the depth of field. A tripod may be required, depending on ambient light, since the camera may choose a slow shutter speed. If using a point-and-shoot camera, you may find this mode helpful for outdoor crime or accident scenes.

- *Macro:* The macro mode is used for close-up photography. If using a point-and-shoot camera, select the macro mode whenever taking a close-up photograph.
- *Sports:* The sports mode allows moving objects to be captured without blur. Fast shutter speeds will be selected. This is a valuable mode if using a point-and-shoot camera on surveillance missions.
- *Program:* Some cameras have a program mode that is distinct from the fully automatic mode. In these cameras, the program mode will offer the photographer a limited ability to adjust settings, including functions such as flash, white balance, and International Organization for Standardization (ISO). The functions of the program mode differ according to camera model; thus, one would be required to review the camera manual. We suggest foregoing the program mode and instead using manual, aperture priority, or shutter priority modes.

Obtaining Quality Crime Scene Images: Concepts and Methods

It is understandably important that a crime scene photograph clearly and accurately represent what you saw at the crime scene. In order to accomplish this common sense objective, we prescribe a few key principles:

- Ensure proper exposure (lighting) and quality of light.
- Ensure that the photograph is sharp by properly focusing the camera, eliminating blur caused by camera movement, and maximizing depth of field.

A closer look at each of these principles will help provide a clear understanding of each. We will also provide simplified methods of accomplishing these, without the use of overburdening and confusing technical jargon.

Exposure and Light Quality

Exposure can be defined simply as the amount of light in a photograph. Generally, the goal will be to generate a well-lit image that is neither too dark nor too light. While there may be a few occasions in which a purposeful underexposure or overexposure would be warranted, in most instances, a balanced exposure will be best. For most crime scenes, this will be relatively straightforward since digital cameras provide immediate feedback. If you encounter exposure problems in your photograph, you can adjust the exposure or flash settings and immediately correct the issue by adding or reducing the amount of light. Your ability to adjust these settings is critical; thus, some fundamental knowledge of exposure settings is required.

Four main camera variables affect exposure: ISO, aperture size (f-stop), shutter speed, and ambient light. With a bit of practice, you will be able to use each of these to achieve the correct amount of light. And if all else fails and you have difficulty manipulating camera settings, we will provide you with a simple method that nearly always results in a proper exposure.

Ambient Light

Ambient light is a term used to describe the existing light at a scene. The first variable you must account for at a scene is the existing light. Subsequent sections in this guide explain which settings should be adjusted and specifically how to adjust them to account for, or take advantage of, the existing light. The fundamental principle, however, is not complicated: You will adjust your camera to maximize its sensitivity to light and/or use a flash unit when ambient light is dim. Conversely, you will maximize the camera settings to minimize sensitivity to light when photographing during times when the ambient light is very bright.

ISO

ISO also affects the amount of light in a photograph. ISO is the common short name for International Organization for Standardization and was a very important factor in photographic film processing. The utility of the ISO setting has carried forward to the digital camera generations; the ISO of a digital camera refers to the camera sensor's sensitivity to light. Most cameras have ISO settings that range from low (below 100) to high (we will define high as anything over 800). We advise that you learn how to adjust the ISO settings on your camera since this will impact both the amount of light and the quality of the image. Since our goal is to keep things simple, we prescribe using a range from 100 to 400 for your crime scene photography. If you are outside on a bright day, 100 will be the prescription. The lower the number of the ISO setting, the less sensitive the camera sensor will be to light. So an ISO 100 will result in an image being less bright than an ISO 400, if all other variables are the same. The advantage of lower ISO numbers lies within the quality of the image: the lower the number, the better the quality. That being said, many crime scenes are photographed at night, or inside with dimly lit scenes;

thus, we would prescribe ISOs of up to 400 for those instances. We believe that so long as you keep your ISO at 400 or lower, you will not compromise the quality of your image to such an extent that it could cause problems for investigative purposes or courtroom admissibility. In fact, the difference in quality between 100 and 400 is generally not noticeable. High ISOs, may present a grainy appearance, especially with older cameras, and should thus be avoided whenever possible. An exception would be for use in surveillance photography, when the use of a flash unit is not practical, or outdoor photography at night, when using painting with light techniques (see Chapter 10).

Aperture/f-Stop

The aperture is an opening in a camera lens that allows light to pass through and strike the camera sensor. Apertures are adjustable; you can make this opening larger/wider or smaller to suit your needs. You can use the aperture to help control the level of light: the smaller the opening, the less light in the image. Conversely, larger apertures create images with more light.

Apertures are expressed in numbers called f-stops. One need not be concerned with the detailed mathematics that serves as the premise for the f-stop numbers; however, you may find it helpful to have a basic understanding of the concept. And you should certainly be able to correlate f-stop numbers with the amount of light that will strike the camera sensor, at least in general terms.

The f-stops are actually fractions of the focal length of the lens. One can determine the actual diameter of the aperture by dividing the lens length by the f-stop. For example, a 50 mm lens and an f-2 would result in a 25 mm aperture size (50/2 = 25). The good news is that there is no actual reason to do this math at a crime scene! We are simply providing this general explanation so you have a better understanding of the f-stop numbers. You simply need to be able to adjust your f-stops in order to control lighting to suit your needs. As you will read in a subsequent section, f-stop selection also serves to affect another key aspect of the photograph as well: depth of field. For now, though, we will focus on its effect on lighting.

You can generally identify the camera's f-stop numbers on camera display panels. This allows photographers to quickly view the f-stop setting so that adjustments can be made quickly and easily. The f-stops range from low numbers, such as f-2, to higher numbers, such as f-32.

Let us take a look at the practical application of f-stops in order to adjust light. *Here is what you really must know:* the lower your f-stop number, the larger the lens opening (aperture), which means more light in your photograph. So an f-2 would allow more light through the lens than an f-4 or an f-8, f-11, f-16, and so on. Conversely, and quite logically, the higher the f-stop number, the less light will be allowed through the lens. So an f-11 would allow less light in an image than an f-8, f-5.6, f-4, and so on. So f-stops run along a continuum from those which allow a high amount of light (lower numbers) to those which allow the least light (higher numbers).

The practical implication of the f-stop is simple: if you require more light in an image, you may select a lower f-stop number. The opposite is also true: simply select a higher f-stop number if you need to reduce the amount of light in an image. For example, let us say you have found that f-16 works well for photographing an outdoor crime scene on a bright, sunny day. But one spot in the scene is shaded, and the result is an underexposed image for that portion of the scene. You can correct this underexposure by selecting a lower f-stop number, such as f-11 or f-8, depending on how deep the shade is.

Because each camera is different, it is difficult for us to provide specific instructions regarding the actual process of adjusting the f-stops. Most cameras have dials or buttons which allow you to change these settings rapidly; you will have to refer to your camera manual. Most manuals have quick reference sections which can save you some time when locating key settings, such as f-stops. In order to gain a level of familiarity and competence with key settings, such as the f-stop, we advise frequent practice with your camera using the manual mode. Take practice images adjusting your shutter speeds and f-stops while noting the effects on the amount of light in the photograph. This practice will not only allow you to gain insight into which settings work well in certain conditions, but also help your level of acuity with your camera dials, buttons, and other features.

Shutter Speed

Cameras have shutters, which open and close when you press the button to take a photograph. The shutter, when open, allows light to reach the camera sensor. So the longer the shutter is open, the higher the volume of light that will strike the camera sensor. Conversely, if a shutter opens and closes very fast, little light will make it to the camera sensor.

The speed at which this shutter opens and closes is called the shutter speed. In general, shutter speeds are fast, usually fractions of a second. Most cameras will display shutter speeds on easy-to-view displays which will allow rapid and easy adjustments. Cameras will generally display shutter speeds as whole numbers, for example, 60, but the number 60 in this example actually represents a fraction of a second. So 60 actually means 1/60th of a second. Exceptions to this include shutter speeds that are one second in length and longer. These are often displayed using the second symbol, which appears as quotes: an example would be 2″, representing a two-second shutter speed. In this case, the shutter opens, stays open for two seconds, then closes. Very slow shutter speeds are generally reserved for low-light photography and other specialized applications that we cover in the later sections of this guide.

The camera's shutter speed is a key factor in exposure and can be adjusted to allow more or less light into the camera sensor, thus allowing you to brighten or dim your image. In order to accomplish this, you will have to form a basic understanding of the shutter speed numbers. If you can simply remember that the higher the shutter speed number displayed, the faster the shutter speed, you will be on track. So a shutter speed of 250 is faster than a 200; remember that these numbers represent fractions (1/250th of a second versus 1/200th of a second). Of course, 1/250th of a second is faster than 1/200th of a second.

To apply this knowledge in practical terms, understand that if you need more light in your image, one option will be to slow down your shutter speed by selecting a lower number. Conversely, if you wish to reduce the light, select a faster shutter speed, represented as a higher number. With this in mind, we highly recommend reading your camera manual to become familiar with specific controls required to adjust your shutter speed. This is usually very easy; you will rotate a dial one direction or another.

Exposure Compensation

Thus far we have described the primary methods of controlling light, or exposure. Although you will often be able to achieve excellent exposure by manipulating the ISO, f-stop, or shutter speed, you might find another method to be easier, depending on the circumstances. This method, or camera function, is called exposure compensation. Exposure compensation is a function that allows you to either reduce or add light in incremental fashion with a click of a button or turn of a dial. This function only operates in the aperture priority, shutter priority, and program shooting modes. We advise you to consult your camera manual to locate the exposure compensation buttons or dials. Once you locate this function, it is quite intuitive—exposure compensation is displayed in either positive or negative numbers. Positive numbers mean an increase in light, while negative numbers mean a reduction in light. We think you will find exposure compensation to be a simple and effective method for fine-tuning exposure.

Bracketing

Speaking of fine-tuning, we advise that you become familiar with a process called bracketing. Bracketing means that in addition to taking a properly exposed image, you would take intentionally slightly underexposed and overexposed images of a particular item of evidence or scene. This is often helpful for forensic examiners, especially those who examine pattern evidence such as fingerprints, tire impressions, footwear impressions, and bite marks. Sometimes, slight overexposures and underexposures tend to better reveal minute details of the evidence. Since it is difficult for the crime scene investigator to know how any particular image will appear when under magnification in a laboratory, bracketing is used, thus allowing a choice of photographs for the examiner to work with. This being said, bracketing is certainly not necessary for every crime scene photograph, or even every item of evidence. Subsequent sections of this guide provide specific guidance regarding when it would be wise to bracket. In addition, many agencies and departments have policies and procedures which may provide concrete guidance.

Several effective methods can be used to properly bracket an image. You will have the option of using the f-stop, shutter speed, or exposure compensation. Ultimately, you will make the decision based on the

FIGURE 3.1 Compare this image with Figure 3.2. You can see the varying levels of exposure. This is called bracketing, which is defined as taking several images of the same scene with different exposure settings.

FIGURE 3.2 This is the same scene as in Figure 3.1, but is a bit more exposed. In this case, the f-stop was adjusted to allow more light through the lens.

lighting conditions, your preference, and secondary effects of adjusting the shutter speeds and f-stops (we describe these secondary effects later in this chapter [covered in the "Obtaining Clear and Sharp Images" section]) (Figures 3.1 and 3.2 are exterior photographs taken with slightly different exposure settings). Figures 3.3 through 3.5 are interior images taken with three different exposure levels.

In addition, many cameras have automatic bracketing, which will allow a series of photographs to be exposed with every touch of the exposure button. You will need to consult with your camera manual to learn how to operate this feature.

Exposure Meters

DSLR cameras have a tool called an exposure meter, which will save you both time and effort in attempting to

FIGURE 3.3 Compare this image with Figures 3.4 and 3.5. Exposure compensation was used to adjust exposure.

FIGURE 3.4 This is the same scene as in Figure 3.3, but is less exposed.

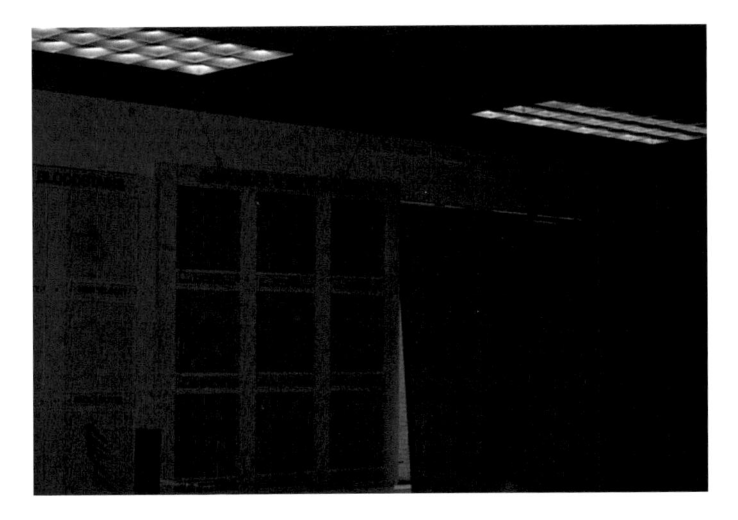

FIGURE 3.5 This is the same scene as in Figures 3.3 and 3.4, but is less exposed.

determine a proper exposure for any given photograph. Cameras with meters will automatically calculate the light requirements and allow you to quickly gauge whether your current camera settings would produce a properly exposed photograph.

Exposure meters can be seen through the camera viewfinder/eyepiece lens when the camera is in manual shooting mode. Most meters have a series of bars that represent segments of light. The center portion of the meter represents a proper exposure. Most will have + or – indicators, which represent whether there is too much or too little light, respectively. So if your camera meter displays a light level of +2 bars, then you will understand that you must reduce the amount of light by two segments. These segments, in the world of photography experts, are referred to as stops of light. Instead of delving into the technical aspects of determining how to calculate an exact stop of light, we suggest simply adjusting your f-stop or shutter speed incrementally while observing the camera meter. You will quickly learn through experience how to properly adjust these settings to correspond to the number of segments shown on the meter.

To use the camera meter, you would focus on an item and then examine the exposure meter. Based on the feedback from the camera meter, you would then make adjustments to your shutter speed or f-stop to ensure proper lighting. For example, if the camera meter suggests that the lighting at the scene will result in an underexposure by two bars, you could change your shutter speed from 250 (1/250th of a second) to 60 (1/60th of a second). Remember that this slower shutter speed time will allow additional light to reach your camera sensor. The camera meter will recognize this and adjust the number of bars accordingly. Once your bars line up with the designated point for a proper exposure, you can be confident, in most instances, that your photograph will be properly exposed.

Most DSLR cameras have a few methods in which the camera meter will function. The common types of meters are averaging/center weighted, spot, and matrix.

Averaging/center weighted meters measure light in the middle of the frame to gauge the proper amount of light. Spot meters measure light from a very specific area of the frame. Matrix meters use a series of grids to determine the proper amount of light for each grid. Although each of the types of meters has advantages, we recommend using the matrix meter for most of your photography since it will provide a more accurate measure of light for the entire photograph. Spot meters might be useful for specific instances, such as surveillance missions, but would otherwise not be recommended. We do not recommend use of averaging/center-weighted meters since matrix meters are generally more effective.

Unusually Lit Scenes

Using the camera light meter, when in manual shooting mode, will certainly save you some time and effort and be effective most of the time. There are occasions, however, when the meters will provide inaccurate results. These scenes are considered unusual or nonnormal scenes and often have wide-ranging amounts of light that cause the camera meters some difficulty in gauging the amount of light in a scene. Most unusual scenes consist of very bright (Figures 3.6 and 3.7) or overly dark (Figures 3.8 and 3.9) environments. When camera meters attempt to gauge the

FIGURE 3.6 This image is underexposed as a result of the camera's light meter being "tricked" by an overly light scene. When you encounter light scenes, you should adjust your exposure to allow more light into the camera sensor.

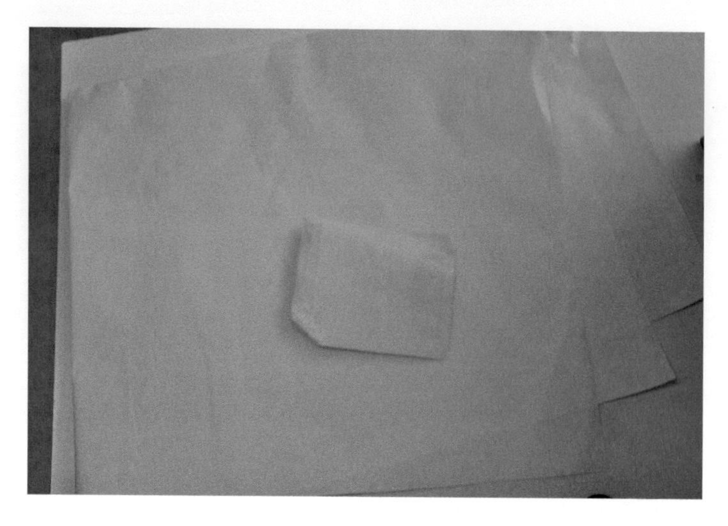

FIGURE 3.7 Same photograph as in Figure 3.6, but with added light.

FIGURE 3.8 A predominantly dark scene may result in an overexposure if you rely upon the camera's automatic metering system. In these instances, you will be required to reduce light through use of the f-stop, shutter speed, or exposure compensation. This image was taken using the camera's metering system as a guide.

FIGURE 3.9 This is the same scene as in Figure 3.8, but adjustments were made to reduce exposure.

light in these unusual scenes, some overcompensation occurs. So, for example, you are photographing a very dark arson scene. Your camera meter detects a very low level of light, too low in fact. So the camera meter will suggest that you add too much light, with the result being an overexposed photograph. So, oddly enough, dark scenes result in overexposures, while very light scenes result in underexposures. Common unusual scenes encountered by investigators include arson scenes, skin (light or dark), scenes with a large amount of sky, snow, or backlit scenes.

To properly photograph unusually lit scenes, we advise a very simple approach. Begin the process as you normally would and then adjust accordingly. If your camera meter indicates that you should have sufficient light in your image but it is actually underexposed, then adjust either your f-stop or shutter speed to allow more light into the photograph. If your entire scene is composed of the same unusual lighting, then additional adjustments may not be necessary.

Some experts recommend metering 18% gray cards which represent a normal scene and then using those gray card-recommended meter settings for the unusually lit portion of the scene. We, however, find it more practical to simply make adjustments as you go based on the feedback of your previous photographs. Since digital cameras offer immediate feedback, you can adjust your camera settings; adding or subtracting light is simple.

Scenes with a high contrast of light and backlit scenes offer unique challenges. Either situation will result in the camera meter providing inaccurate results since there is such a high contrast in the amount of light between different portions of the image. You will generally end up with one portion of your image being properly exposed, while another portion is vastly under- or overexposed. The best method of correcting this problem is to use flash, or even a flashlight, to add light to the portions of the scene that are underexposed. This is often called fill flash since the flash (or flashlight) is used to fill in the dark areas of the image.

Exposure Summary

As you can probably surmise, there are several different variables to consider when attempting to determine proper exposure for any given image. Although this might initially seem to be a daunting task, with a bit of practice, you will be able to obtain proper exposure in your photographs in very little time. Making the necessary adjustments will quickly become second nature.

Flash

For many dimly lit crime scenes, no matter what adjustments you make with the f-stop, shutter speed, or exposure compensation, you will not be able to achieve a proper exposure—there just will not be enough ambient light. Your most effective option will be the use of a flash unit. There are many types and models of flash; we will discuss these in general terms and provide some practical advice to help you understand some seemingly complicated technical terms and processes associated with the use of flash. Figures 3.10 and 3.11 depict common detachable flash units.

First, it is important to distinguish between built-in flash units and those which are detachable. Many DSLR cameras have built-in flashes, which are very simple to use and sometimes automatically pop up and function when insufficient light is available. The simplicity of built-in flashes is their only advantage,

FIGURE 3.10 This image depicts a common detachable flash unit.

FIGURE 3.11 This is another image of a common detachable flash unit.

however. These types of flash units are not very powerful; you will usually be able to illuminate only a relatively small area with them. Another problem is that they usually cannot be rotated, so the flash is always directed straight ahead. On many occasions, you will find that this direct light will cause areas of overexposure, or hotspots, which appear as bright spots in the image. These often occur in close-up photographs, which, of course, require visibility of fine details. Another problem with the pop-up flash is the shadow which can be created by the lens when using the pop-up flash. With these weaknesses of built-in flash units in mind, our first bit of practical advice is to disregard built-in flash units altogether and use detachable flash systems whenever possible.

Detachable flash units come in a variety of models; it will be important for you to choose wisely. When purchasing a detachable flash, make sure that the flash unit is compatible with your camera. The power of the flash unit is also a critical factor; more powerful units will provide a larger area of coverage. A flash unit's guide number is a measure of its power. The higher the guide number, the more powerful the flash. We recommend you use a flash unit with a guide number of at least 80, though 120 or above would be a better option. This level of power will ensure that you have adequate flash coverage for larger crime scenes. Ideally, you should be able to illuminate a 40- to 50-foot long area without using extreme apertures, and using higher guide number flash units will help ensure this.

When using your camera and flash, a function called sync speed will help ensure proper exposure. Each camera model has a specific shutter speed designated as its sync speed. This is the fastest shutter speed that should be used when flash is utilized. This will ensure the shutter is completely open for the full duration of the flash. If you use a shutter speed that is higher than the sync speed, the shutter will close as the flash is still firing, thus causing your image to be fully or partially underexposed. Fast shutter speeds have only two purposes: to reduce light and eliminate blur. Since flash is generally used in low-light conditions, including virtually all indoor scenes, there will, of course, be no reason to reduce light further—the goal of using flash is to add light. Secondly, the use of flash will also help prevent blur caused by camera shake, thus minimizing the second reason for the selection of a fast shutter speed. So with this in mind, you can see that there is no purpose for you to exceed the camera's sync speed while using flash. A pragmatic and simple offering of advice is that when using flash, set your shutter speed to sync speed—and leave it there. There is no reason to change it.

To locate your camera's sync speed, consult your flash and/or camera manual. You may also be able to view a graphic representation of it on your display pane when scrolling through shutter speeds. Some manufacturers have a diagram of a flash located adjacent to the appropriate shutter speed selection to represent the sync speed. This may not be visible unless your flash is attached and in the "on" position.

Flash Controls and Functions

Some terms and concepts associated with flash photography can seem confusing. Most high-quality flash units have display panels that provide various information to the photographer. Once you gain experience, you will be able to use this information to help you select the proper settings to maximize your efficiency in obtaining the correct exposure. We will break down some of these processes in a general manner, but more importantly, we will provide some straightforward, pragmatic advice to help you use flash if you do not have a full understanding of all the functions and capabilities.

Flash Modes

Flash units have various modes which dictate how the flash will operate and how much of the control will be handled by the camera/flash itself instead of you, the operator. If you are a novice, then selecting modes which allow the camera and flash unit to make some decisions automatically will be very helpful.

The three flash modes most essential to crime scene photography are through the lens (TTL), automatic, and manual. Both TTL and automatic allow the camera and flash unit to automate much of the decision-making. We estimate that you will be able to use these modes for three-quarters or more of your crime scene flash photography work.

The TTL mode is also referred to as dedicated flash. TTL operates through the use of a sensor in the camera which measures the amount of light reflected back from the flash. In other words, the flash unit will fire and the flash will reflect off of objects in your scene back through the camera lens and finally strike the sensor. Once the camera's processor determines that sufficient light is obtained, the flash will discontinue. This mode is very helpful in preventing overexposed images and gives you a wide range of distances in which the flash will be effective. This range will depend somewhat on your f-stop selection. Remember that the f-stop corresponds to the opening in the camera that allows light to pass (called the aperture), so a higher f-stop number, such as f-22, would provide a smaller effective exposure range than an f-8. For example, an f-8 may provide you with an effective exposure range of 2–45 feet, while an f-22 may cover only 3–15 feet.

Because of the ability of TTL to help mitigate overexposures and the freedom it provides you to work within various distance ranges, we recommend that you use TTL for the majority of crime scene photography. This is especially true if you are a novice. You will save both time and effort, since you will be spared the difficulty of constantly changing your f-stop to ensure a proper exposure.

If your flash unit does not have a TTL mode, the best option for novices is the automatic mode. The automatic mode functions in a similar manner as TTL does; the primary difference is that the sensor which measures the reflected light is located on the flash unit, instead of inside the camera. As such, it is less precise in measuring proper exposure settings, so you will likely have to fine-tune your f-stops for some of your images. Also, since the sensor is located on the flash unit, you will find a significant decrease in accuracy in measuring exposure when your flash unit is detached from the camera.

The manual flash mode leaves exposure control decisions to the photographer. This mode allows the most discretion and ability to control variables, but requires the highest level of technical aptitude. Unless you have a sufficient level of technical expertise, we recommend that you reserve the use of the manual flash mode for very specific purposes. If you attempt to photograph your entire scene by using the manual flash mode, you will find it necessary to make constant adjustments to your f-stops, or other functions, to ensure proper exposures.

The specific situations in which we recommend the manual flash mode involve unusually lit scenes. Some scenes, as previously mentioned, may cause your camera some difficulty in metering light. If you find that the TTL or automatic mode is not providing proper exposures (too dark or too light), then you can switch to the manual mode. Once on manual mode, retake the photograph while paying attention to your f-stop selections. Once you determine whether you need more or less light, simply adjust your f-stop accordingly. For example, if you use f-8 on your first photograph and it is overexposed, you could switch to f-11 on the next photograph. With just a bit of practice, you will quickly be able to fine-tune your f-stop selections to match the ambient light at the scene.

A few other unusual situations exist in which we advise the consideration of using the manual flash mode. When you are confronted with a scene with a high contrast of light, you might use fill flash (see Figures 3.12 and 3.13) to fill in the dark areas with a

FIGURE 3.12 This image was taken without fill flash.

FIGURE 3.13 This image was taken with fill flash.

proper amount of light. You will find that manual flash is often effective for this purpose. Also, when you wish to use bounce light (described in detail in the "Bounce Flash" section), manual flash is often best.

Off-Camera Flash

There will be occasions when it is preferable to remove your flash unit from the camera and hold it in other positions. You will attach your flash unit to a cable and then attach the other end of the cable to the camera (see Figure 3.14). By using the flash cable and detached flash unit, you can alter the angle of the flash and allow yourself more flexibility in illuminating the subject matter. With some experience, you will quickly be able to identify when this would be preferred. We recommend considering it when photographing items with curved surfaces; when the normal, direct flash

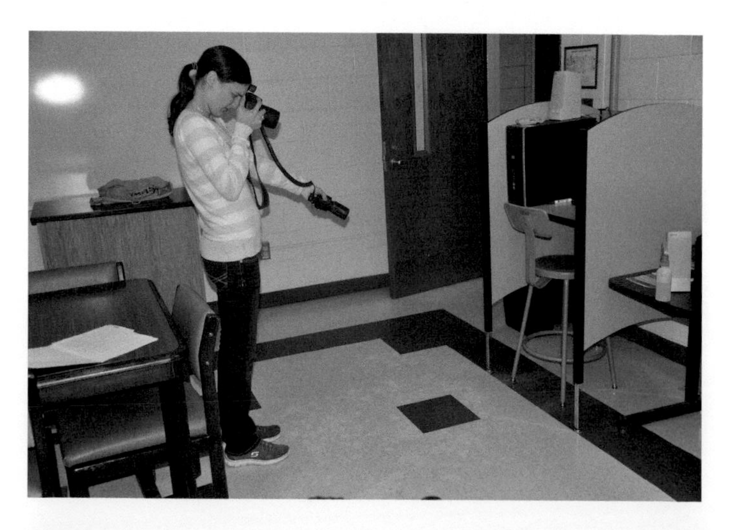

FIGURE 3.14 This image depicts the use of an off-camera flash to properly expose a dark area within an otherwise well-lit scene. This is referred to as fill flash or fill-in flash.

FIGURE 3.15 This image depicts a photographer illuminating a curved surface by using off-camera flash.

causes hotspots; and when oblique lighting is preferred. Oblique lighting is further detailed in Chapters 8 and 9.

Curved surfaces are often difficult to illuminate evenly due to the uneven surface. Therefore, direct flash often results in portions of the image being underexposed since the flash will not directly strike all surfaces. You will find that by using a flash cable and holding your flash in alternate positions, you will be able to more evenly light all areas of the curved surface (see Figure 3.15). You should anticipate a bit of trial and error with this technique, but as with many other techniques, with just a bit of practice, you will find this quite simple.

Bounce Flash

You might also find that using direct flash causes distinctly bright spots in your image. These are caused by the flash itself and are usually located in the center area of the images, or where highly reflective surfaces are located. If your flash unit does not allow the flash head to be rotated away from the 90° angle position, your best bet will be to use an off-camera flash and bounce the light. Either way, if you aim the flash in different directions, instead of straight at the subject matter, you will allow the light to bounce off of other items. This will cause the light to be diffused and create a softer, more balanced illumination of the subject matter. This is a common flash diffusion technique called bounce flash (Figure 3.16 depicts a photographer using bounce flash). Keep in mind that the flash must travel a longer distance, so manual flash may be more effective than TTL or automatic. You also may need to select a larger aperture by maneuvering your f-stop to a lower number. So if you were using an f-11 in your initial direct flash photograph,

FIGURE 3.16 This image depicts a photographer using bounce light to dissipate the flash, thus avoiding hotspots.

you might find that an f-8 is more effective when bouncing the light. The further your light must travel from the object you are bouncing it from, the larger the aperture you will need. We find that bouncing light off ceilings is highly effective for many situations that require flash diffusion. We also recommend considering bouncing your light in other directions as well, depending on the nature of your scene. One more thing to keep in mind when using bounce flash is the color of the surface used to bounce the light. The light from a colored surface may cause the photograph to take on the color of that surface. White or off-white/gray surfaces will produce the best results. Lastly, bounce flash is not generally a technique used outdoors. While you can bounce the flash off an index card or built-in bounce card, there is too much light lost to be effective when pointing the flash head away from the subject. Ultimately each scene is unique; thus, training and practice will help you refine this technique. One downside to using bounce flash is its impact on batteries and flash recycle times. Because more light is required from the flash, the batteries are drained more quickly and the flash will need more time between photographs to charge to full capacity. Figures 3.17 through 3.19 illustrate how bounce flash can be used to improve your photographs.

Other Flash Diffusion Techniques

Several techniques are available, in addition to bounce light, to help reduce the intensity of flash and thus reduce overexposures and hotspots. A few of these techniques will be described, those which we have found most useful and practical.

FIGURE 3.17 This image was taken with direct flash. You can see the hotspot caused by the flash.

FIGURE 3.18 This was taken with bounce flash; you can notice the reduction in glare caused by the removal of the direct flash.

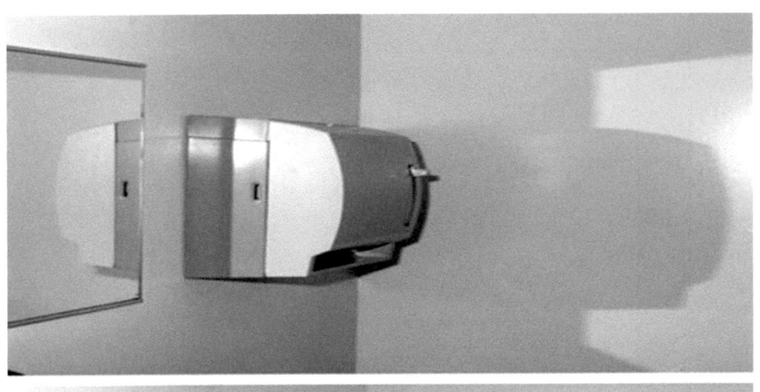

FIGURE 3.19 These images depict how bounce flash can reduce shadows caused by direct flash. The top image was taken with direct flash, and the bottom image was taken with bounce flash.

Many flash units are equipped with a plastic cover, called a diffuser (Figure 3.20), which can be placed over the actual flash source. This diffuser, in addition to protecting the flash unit, serves to soften the flash. It is handy since the cover will fit securely and not require you to hold it in place. These devices can be very useful indoors, creating a very even lighting without the need to continually adjust the flash to bounce against a nearby surface.

Another effective technique is the placement of a tissue or piece of paper over the flash unit. This may, however, limit your flexibility since you will have

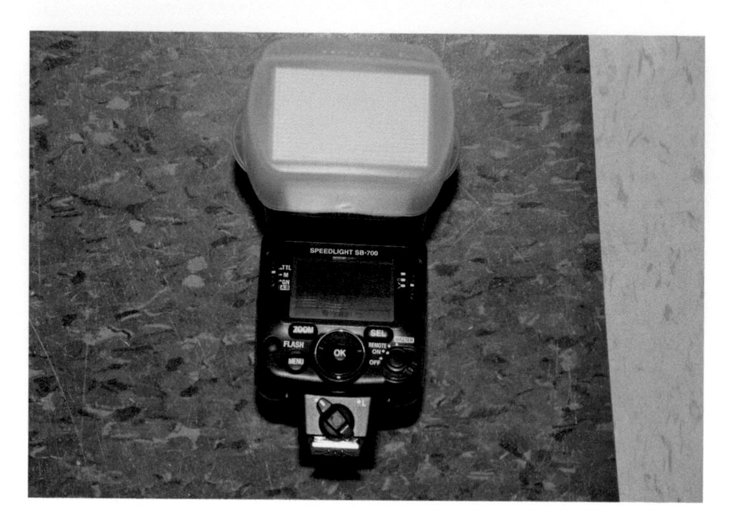

FIGURE 3.20 This is a diffuser cap that fits over detachable flash units.

to hold the tissue or paper in place. You should find that you are able to adjust the actual level of flash intensity by using more or less tissue or paper. Simply doubling up the tissue or paper is an effective method of further reducing the light. We recommend this technique primarily because of its expediency and simplicity. No fancy, expensive equipment is required, and it takes very little practice to realize its benefit and utility. It may serve as a useful field-expedient method for those times when you do not have the necessary equipment immediately available.

If your agency has an ample budget and you can afford quality accessories for your camera, we advise purchasing a ring flash. A ring flash is a different type of flash that is shaped in a circle, or ring. You would use a ring flash in lieu of the regular flash unit. Ring flashes work very well in illuminating objects softly and evenly, generally eliminating hotspots. We think you will find ring flash units highly effective for close-up work since soft light and elimination of glare and hotspots is critical in order to capture the fine details associated with close-up photography. In addition to ring flashes, you might find the use of specially designed close-up flash units to be a useful accessory for your photography kits. Just like the ring flash, these units will require you to attach the flash to your camera before taking photographs. These units have similar advantages to ring flashes; they serve to evenly distribute light and help reduce glare and hotspots.

Although not considered diffusion techniques, most medium- to higher-priced flash units have built-in methods for adjusting the intensity of the flash. These methods do not actually cause the light to spread out, or diffuse, but do serve to reduce, or increase, the intensity of light. And they do so in a quick, easy manner once you are able to master the functions and controls on your camera and flash unit.

When using the manual flash mode, many flash units have variable power settings which allow you to reduce or increase the intensity of the flash with a touch of a button. This button will be found on the flash unit itself. Adjustments to the power output are usually displayed as fractions on the flash display. Since there is such a large selection of flash units available, we suggest that you review your flash unit manual to determine if your flash unit has variable power settings. If so, spend a few minutes to determine how to use this powerful function. Again, it is not a complicated process and well worth the few minutes of research and practice.

A second relatively easy method of adjusting the exposure when using flash is using flash exposure compensation. Some cameras have buttons for this function;

some are controlled through the flash, and some have both. We, again, suggest that you review your camera and flash manuals to locate the buttons or dials responsible for controlling flash exposure compensation.

Flash exposure compensation works in the same manner as exposure compensation does—you can either add or reduce light by pressing the buttons and rotating the dials on your camera and/or flash. So you will be able to easily adjust the amount of light without having to change your shutter speeds and f-stops. This can be an effective time saver. Flash exposure compensation will function with TTL and automatic flash modes, but not with manual flash mode. The exposure changes you can make will be reflected as +1, +2, +3, −1, −2, −3, and so on. The positive numbers reflect that your photograph will have more light, and the reverse is true for the negative numbers. Each whole

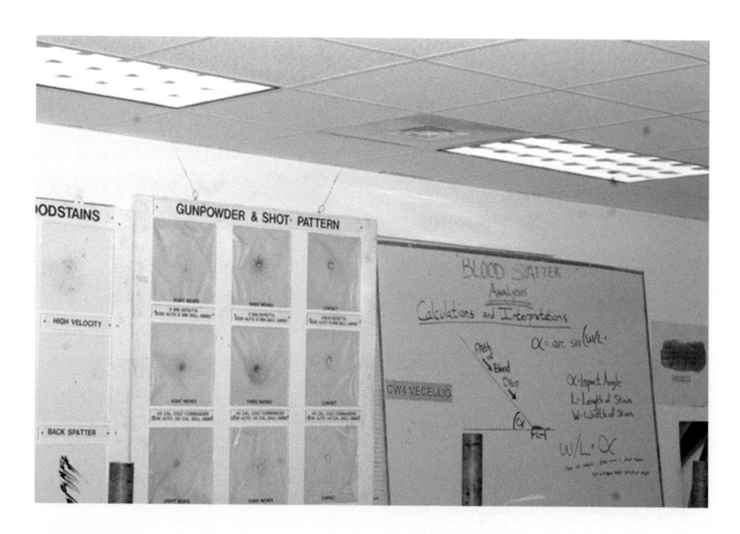

FIGURE 3.21 This image was taken using detachable flash unit. The EV was adjusted to +2. Contrast this image with Figure 3.22.

number represents a halving or doubling of light. So, for instance, moving from a +1 to +2 will double the amount of light. Moving from -2 to -1 will reduce light by half.

Your flash unit may also display the letters *EV*, which is short for exposure value (EV). The EV reflects the same information as the flash exposure compensation. Just like exposure flash compensation, if you see an EV of -1, that would mean that there would be half the light in your image from the normal flash setting (which would be displayed as zero). A -2 EV means the light would be reduced by one half again, so now the total light would be one-fourth of that in the normally exposed image. A positive number means a doubling of light; +1 is double that of zero, +2 doubles the light again, and so on. Figures 3.21 and 3.22 are images in which the EV was adjusted.

FIGURE 3.22 This image is the same scene as in Figure 3.21, but with an EV of -2.

Obtaining Clear and Sharp Images

To ensure that your crime scene images meet your objectives of being suitable for later investigative analysis or use in the courtroom, you must, in addition to ensuring proper exposure, be able to take photographs that are in focus and free of blur caused by motion. In order to achieve this sharpness and high degree of clarity, it will be important to master the tasks of focusing your camera and maximizing the range of your image that is actually in focus.

Properly Focusing the Camera

You can focus DSLR cameras in one of two primary methods: manually and automatically. Some less expensive cameras may not have a manual focus option, so if you are using such a model, then, of course, the choice is made for you. DSLR cameras, however, allow you the flexibility of focusing the camera yourself. We strongly recommend learning to use this feature; it will benefit you tremendously in certain situations. Some photographers, in fact, rely on manual focus for all their crime scene photography. We urge you to practice and determine which method is best for you and garner the skill to use both methods. We will provide some pros and cons of each method as well as describe certain occasions in which one method will be preferable over the other.

Manual control, as you may surmise, allows you to focus without assistance from the camera. In order to accomplish this, you will need to ensure that your camera and lens are both set to allow manual focus. This is often represented as an *M* on a selector switch, but we advise you to consult with your camera manual if the focus selector is not plainly visible. Once your camera and lens are set to manual focus, you will then turn the focal ring to actually focus the lens. Some novices may initially confuse the focal ring with the zoom function, so beware—the focal ring will not move your lens in and out, causing objects to appear larger or smaller—that is the zoom function. Focal rings are smaller and may be located at either end of a zoom lens.

The primary advantage you will gain from manually focusing the camera is precision. You, not the camera, know which portion of the scene, or which object within the scene, is of primary importance. By using manual focus, you can focus on these specific areas, or objects, to ensure that they are captured clearly. This may be especially important in close-up photography involving key items of evidence when it may be critical to achieve perfect focus on small, fine details. You may also find manual focus very useful in scenes that have objects located at various distances within your focal area. By using manual focus, you can focus on the objects that are most important, or in a certain area that would maximize your ability to ensure that all the objects are in focus. If you defer to autofocus, you will, to some extent, be at the mercy of the camera. You will also be able to use a technique to maximize the range of your photograph that is in clear focus, called depth of field, which we discuss in detail in the "Depth of Field" section.

From reading the aforementioned advice, you might infer that we do not recommend autofocus, but that is just not the case. Autofocus, if properly used, can be effective and save you an extensive amount of time and effort. We submit that the time-saving aspect of using autofocus is its primary positive attribute. Instead of taking several seconds to properly focus your image as is the case with using manual focus, your camera will automatically focus very quickly, sometimes imperceptibly fast. Since you will often capture hundreds of images at a crime scene, using autofocus will be a meaningful time-saver.

To use autofocus, you will have to ensure that your selector switch for both the camera and lens are set to autofocus. This is often represented as an *A* or an *AF;* check your camera manual to be sure. Once the autofocus function is set, the camera will do the focusing work for you. All you have to do is orient your camera to focus on an object, and the camera will do the rest. Some cameras may require you to partially depress the shutter release button (the button that actually takes the photograph) in order to trigger the autofocus function.

Autofocus is generally recommended for overall crime scene photographs, especially those that do not have objects located at varying distances. For instance, photographing the exterior of a residence is often easily and effectively accomplished with autofocus, especially if there are no intermediary objects.

Problems with autofocus may include focusing on scenes with objects at various distances, as mentioned previously, as well as same-colored, plain backgrounds, particularly when they are white. Cameras often have difficulty sensing homogenous backgrounds and simply will not focus. We simply recommend using manual focus in these instances.

The selection of autofocus versus manual focus will often depend on your preference, so practice with each and use what works best for you. We have provided some pros and cons of each, so with just a bit of practice, your focus selection will become second nature.

Preventing Blur through Shutter Speed Selection

In addition to controlling exposure, shutter speeds are also used to eliminate blur. First, it is important to understand that blurry photographs may be caused by a few different things. First, camera shake, even very subtle movement, will result in blur if your shutter speed is not set properly. Second, blur can be caused by moving objects.

A few methods are available to prevent camera shake. The first is stabilization through use of a tripod. Although certainly effective, using a tripod for every crime scene photograph is impractical. We would recommend using a tripod when necessary, such as for examination-quality close-up photographs. For the majority of your photographs, however, camera shake can be controlled through the selection of a proper shutter speed.

To accomplish this, there are two basic rules that must be followed. Each of these rules relate to the lens length.

- Rule 1: Select a shutter speed that is equal to, or higher, than the lens focal length.
- Rule 2: Avoid shutter speeds below 60 (1/60th of a second).

In order to implement these rules, you will need to determine the lens length. Some lenses have static lengths, and you will easily be able to locate the lens length on the lens itself. Other lenses have a range of lengths; these are referred to as zoom lenses since they can zoom in or out, causing objects to appear closer (telephoto lenses: above 50 mm in length) or further away (wide-angle lenses: below 50 mm in length). Zoom lenses generally have a range of lens length numbers printed on them. You will identify the length of the lens by observing the number that aligns with a designator on the lens, which is usually a white dot or line. Once you identify the specific lens length you are using, ensure that your shutter speed numbers are equal to, or higher, than that particular lens length. Since zoom lenses are adjustable, it may be advisable to select a shutter speed with a higher number than the longest length (highest number) within the range of your lens. This will prevent you from being compelled to adjust your shutter speed for each photograph. For example, if you are using an 18–105 mm zoom lens, you can select a shutter speed equal to or higher than 105. Since shutter speeds are incremental, you will find that the next highest shutter speed is 125. If you choose a shutter speed of 125 and use that for all your photographs, the chances of blur caused by camera shake will be minimized, no matter the length of the lens you use.

Remember that shutter speed is one of a few variables that affect exposure, so if you use a relatively fast shutter speed to prevent blur, you will have to compensate for the reduction in light. In many cases, the use of a flash unit would be the preferred option. Using a flash unit will allow you to have adequate lighting while avoiding the use of a large aperture, which will create problems with depth of field Remember that we recommend selecting the camera's sync shutter speed when using flash.

Some photographs, such as photographs of fingerprints or footwear impressions, will often require low lighting or specialized light sources. In these cases, slow shutter speeds will often be mandatory to ensure proper lighting. In these, and in any other circumstances in which you would rather use a slow shutter speed, the use of a tripod will be required. Tripods will keep your camera stable enough to prevent blur caused by camera shake. In subsequent sections of this guide, we provide additional instructions for specialized techniques that require a tripod.

Depth of Field

In addition to focusing your camera and eliminating blur through the proper selection of shutter speed, you can also control the range of your photograph that is in proper focus. Depth of field is defined as the distance, from the foreground to the background, of the image that is actually in sharp focus. You have probably seen photographs in which the primary subject is in focus, but all of the scene in front of (foreground) and behind (background) of the primary object is blurry, a technique often used in portrait photography. This is considered a shallow depth of field since only a short range of the image is in focus. In the field of crime scene photography, unlike artistic photography, there is no reason to intentionally blur any portion of an image. In fact, doing so could potentially make you susceptible to courtroom attacks on the admissibility of the image and/or your competence/credibility. The objective should be to maximize depth of field, thereby ensuring as much of your photograph as possible is clear and sharp. Fortunately, there are a few relatively easy methods you can employ to assure that you can maximize the depth of field.

Using your f-stop to maximize depth of field is a relatively straightforward method that will have a direct impact on the depth of field. Lower-numbered f-stops that result in wide apertures result in poor, or shallow, depth of field. Higher-numbered f-stops that result in narrow apertures result in better, or longer, depth of field. There are other factors which we will explain, but all else being the same, a higher-numbered f-stop will provide a better depth of field than a lower-numbered f-stop. Figures 3.23 and 3.24 reveal how the f-stop setting can be used to improve the depth of field.

With this in mind, we recommend avoiding f-stops below f-8 whenever possible. There may be an occasional use for wider apertures, but this should generally be limited to low-light, specialized techniques such as those involving fluorescence and luminescence. Generally, you should be able to keep your f-stops above f-8. In order to accomplish this, it is important to understand how other exposure variables tie in. Since your goal is to use relatively narrow apertures (f-stops above f-8), you will want to maximize exposure by adjusting your other settings.

First, remember that lower ISOs tend to produce higher-quality images. Try to keep the ISO at 400 or less, but in instances where more light is needed,

FIGURE 3.23 This image has a poor (narrow) depth of field which was caused by the use of a wide aperture (low f-stop number). Notice that a significant portion of the image is blurry.

FIGURE 3.24 This image, in contrast to Figure 3.23, has a better depth of field. A small f-stop was used, creating a narrower aperture, resulting in better depth of field. Notice that the majority of the image is in focus.

consider using a higher ISO to get the correct exposure. So, in instances of low light, unless you are taking specialized photographs of critical evidence, we recommend using ISO 400. By doing so, you will allow more light into your image than if you were to choose a lower number ISO setting. The second key variable is shutter speed. Remember that shutter speed prevents blur in addition to managing exposure. Your goal is simple: set the shutter speed as slow as you can while still preventing blur from camera shake. Remember that this will depend on the length of the lens you use as well as whether the subject of your photograph is moving. Choosing the slowest possible shutter speed while still avoiding blur will allow the camera to select the smallest possible aperture and still maximize the amount of light that can be captured in your photograph.

These methods of increasing available light will allow you to select higher f-stop numbers, thus improving your depth of field. That is the goal: maximize the depth of field through the proper control of your exposure settings. This is a relatively easy task when photographing well-lit scenes, but a bit more challenging in low-light conditions. Remember that in these situations, a suitable flash unit should be used. If you use a moderate- or high-powered flash, then you will have no problems using f-stops higher than f-8.

We offer a couple of pragmatic tips to help you with the task of maximizing the depth of field through the control of exposure settings. Instead of adjusting your shutter speed for every photograph, you can allow the camera to do some of the work for you. In order to accomplish this, we will turn to the shutter and aperture priority shooting modes.

Using the shutter priority mode, you can select a suitable shutter speed which will prevent blur from camera shake or object motion. The shutter speed number displayed on your camera (not the actual fraction) should be higher than the length of your lens and should generally not fall below 60, regardless of the lens length. In addition, some cameras display a symbol depicting that your setting will result in camera shake. Once you select the appropriate shutter speed to prevent blur, the camera will select the appropriate f-stop based on ambient light. If your camera selects an f-stop below f-8, then you can use flash to increase light, thus allowing you to select a higher-numbered f-stop.

Aperture priority mode can be used in a similar fashion, although you will have to pay particular attention to the shutter speed to prevent blur from camera shake. You will find aperture priority most useful in well-lit scenes or when using flash, so you do not have to constantly pay attention to the shutter speed. In both of these situations (well-lit scenes and when using flash), you will have sufficient light allowing you to select an f-stop of f-8 or higher without much concern given to the camera selecting slow shutter speeds that could cause blur.

Another effective technique in achieving an acceptable depth of field involves the use of the manual shooting mode. When using TTL flash, you can select f-8 and the sync shutter speed to gain a proper exposure. Although, of course, you will find that there will be scenes or specific shots which require you to use different flash techniques, you will find that this simple method is very effective for much of your work.

Auto Shooting Mode Causes Inferior Depth of Field

We generally do not recommend the use of the fully automatic shooting mode function for crime scene photography. The reason is straightforward: the camera will nearly always select relatively wide apertures. This is a built-in "safety" mechanism that virtually assures proper exposure, but at the cost of a severely reduced depth of field. So unless you are incapable of adjusting f-stops and shutter speeds, or using the other shooting modes, we suggest that you forego the use of the auto mode, instead relying on aperture priority, shutter priority, or manual. Each of these modes, as we have detailed, will allow you to select smaller apertures (higher f-stops) that will allow you to achieve a better depth of field.

Focusing Techniques to Improve Depth of Field

Two focusing methods exist to help maximize depth of field: focusing by the rule of thirds and hyperfocal focusing. The rule of thirds is a zone focusing technique used in scenes that have end points, or barriers. Hyperfocal focusing is used when there is no end to the photograph, or when infinity is in focus.

Whenever a barrier is present, such as any indoor crime scene, focusing about one-third of the distance into your scene will allow you to achieve the best possible depth of field. This is because the depth of field for any given photographs ranges from one-third before the focal point to two-thirds behind it. So focusing one-third into the scene will allow the greatest range of your image to be in clear focus. This will likely take some time to become accustomed to; we have found that most novices intuitively focus on the end point or the primary subject. You may find that manual focus is necessary in some instances in order to accomplish this. You will find that mastering this technique will dramatically improve the quality of your images.

Hyperfocal focusing should be employed for scenes with no direct end point or any scene that exceeds about 80 feet in length. This will generally include some outdoor crime scenes and accident scenes. Hyperfocal focusing is a method which maximizes depth of field, when infinity is the focus point. Most medium- to high-end lenses will have a symbol for infinity on the lens. To perform hyperfocal focusing, you will rotate your lens until the hyperfocal focus symbol is visualized or lined up with a designator on the lens. The actual range of the depth of field will vary, based on your f-stop, camera sensor size, and lens length, but in all cases, the immediate foreground in front of the photographer will not be in clear focus. For example, let us say that you are using an f-16 with a 24 mm lens. You focus using the hyperfocal focusing technique and are able to obtain a depth of field range of 13 feet to infinity. If you then change to an f-8, your range would decrease; the range would now be about 25 feet to infinity (keep in mind that these are estimates and the actual range will depend on the sensor size and crop factors of your camera).

We provide this very basic explanation to introduce you to this technique. For additional reading on the topic, please refer to Edward M. Robinson's book, *Crime Scene Photography*.

危機

CHAPTER 4

Crime Scene Photography

An Overview and Checklist

The following outline provides a quick reference which outlines the specific procedure for photographing crime scenes. Although more detailed descriptions of each step are provided in subsequent sections, we think you may find this outline to be very helpful for refreshing your memory or for those times when you need a brief reminder of certain processes, steps, or tips.

Our methodology follows a least intrusive to most intrusive pattern by beginning with photographs that document the scene in general terms and then by paying particular attention to items of evidence and other key features. You will find that following this methodology will allow you to thoroughly photograph any crime scene, regardless of the nature of the crime. Although the types of evidence found in different types of crime will certainly differ, we believe that by following our standardized, methodological approach you will be able to thoroughly photograph the scene in a manner which will maximize the value of your photographs for courtroom or later investigative purposes. As you might imagine, however, attempting to determine the specific location and purpose of each photograph may be difficult if one is attempting to analyze the photographs months, and, in some cases, years, after the photographs were taken to.

An important step that will help alleviate this problem is the use of a photograph log or memo sheet. The purpose of this document is to memorialize each photograph taken at the crime scene. The log or memo sheet, if properly constructed, will be extremely useful for investigators who later examine photographs for investigative purposes. A proper log or memo sheet should contain the following data: name of photographer, date, case number, type of photograph (overall, mid-range, close-up), and what the photograph is specifically depicting. So, for example, the log may display that photographs 1–5 are overalls of the north wall of the crime scene. We also recommend that the photographer document any additional important notes regarding the photograph that might be important to the investigation. One such example might be that a particular photograph depicted a witness-perspective view. By specifically documenting this in your log, you will avoid later frustration and difficulty locating these noteworthy photographs. You can see an example photograph log/memo sheet in Figure 4.1. Figures 4.2 through 4.4 are crime scene photographs showing different perspectives of a bullet trajectory. It is vital to thoroughly document the purpose of photographs such as these, which may lend profound insight into important elements of the crime.

The typed form is simple and straightforward and can be accomplished on computer terminal in a patrol vehicle. Commercially available preprinted forms are

Names Date ________ Time ____

Case #

Photo #	Type of Photo (overall/360, midrange/perspective/evidence establishing, closeup, close up with scale)	Depicting

FIGURE 4.1 This is a sample photograph log or memo sheet. We believe in keeping a simple log that is not burdensome to complete. The purpose of this log is to help refresh your memory if you need to later review the images for investigative or courtroom purposes. Since digital image files contain camera settings such as f-stop, shutter speed, lens, and ISO, there is no purpose in spending your time documenting this type of data.

FIGURE 4.2 This image may not fall neatly into the prescribed categories of overalls, mid-range, or close-ups. Depicted is an image showing a trajectory rod used to show the path of a bullet in a shooting investigation.

FIGURE 4.3 This image depicts the same trajectory rod as Figure 4.2, but from a different perspective. Different perspective views may be taken for a variety of purposes; it is important to indicate the purpose of the images in your photograph log or memo sheet.

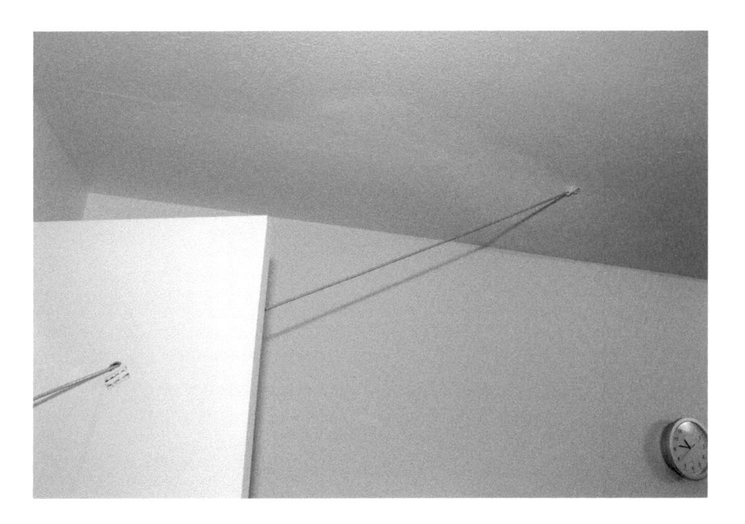

FIGURE 4.4 Another view of the same scene depicted in Figures 4.1 and 4.2 but from another perspective. This image helps to illustrate that several different perspectives should be considered when photographing key items of evidence.

available from forensic supply companies and are simple to use. Even a blank piece of paper with the information handwritten on it will accomplish the task of identifying the series of photographs pertaining to a particular case. The case identifier photograph is especially important when images from multiple scenes will be stored on a single piece of storage media (Figure 4.5).

Checklist

1. Overall photographs

   Objective: To thoroughly photograph the entire crime scene, including entrance and exit points and witness, suspect, or victim perspectives

   - Your first crime scene photograph should be a case identifier, which simply depicts your

Case number: 2016-00256

Photographed by: D. Wilson

Agency: Murfeesboro County Sheriff's office

Date/time: 15 February, 2016 0330

Address: 2345 South Oak street, Unincorporated Musfeesboro County, Texas

FIGURE 4.5 This is just one example of a case identifier photograph.

case number and/or other identifying data required by your agency. Your agency may have a form for this purpose. If not, case identifiers are available through commercial forensic retailers, or you could simply place the information on a piece of paper, index card, or other suitable surface.

- Ensure that your photographs are slightly overlapping and cover the entire scene; this will generally include all rooms in a residential scene.
- Establish the location of the scene by photographing a reference point with the scene in the background.
- Consider taking photographs during the initial walk through or scan of the scene.
- Make sure to take both outdoor and indoor overall photographs for indoor scenes (i.e., make sure to photograph the exterior and curtilage of residences).
- Consider photographing ceilings in indoor scenes.

- Try to align yourself at a 90° angle with the surface you are photographing (in other words, try to avoid diagonal shots).
- A zoom lens is preferable and will provide some flexibility, allowing you to achieve a wider perspective if necessary.

2. Mid-range photographs

Objective: To illustrate spatial relationships between items of evidence with reference points or other key features

- Ensure that at least one mid-range photograph of each item of evidence is exposed.
- Form a triangle with yourself as one vertex, the evidence as another, and a reference point as a third. You should be an equal distance between the evidence and the reference point.
- Focus on an area midway between the evidence and reference points to reduce spatial distortion.
- Ensure that the evidence is framed on one edge of your camera's viewfinder and the reference point is on the opposite edge. This will help reduce spatial distortion.
- Use of a normal lens or focal length that approximates the human field of view is advised since this will reduce distortion. Normal lens lengths vary; you should consult with the lens/camera manufacturer to obtain this.
- Other lens lengths may be used when it is not practical to use a normal lens. In these cases, it is extremely important to frame the evidence and reference point on opposite sides of the viewfinder, as mentioned earlier.

3. Close-up photographs

   Objective: To photograph items of evidence or other key features in a manner which allows the fine details of that item to be clearly visualized

   - When it is necessary to obtain very close images, use a close-up lens specifically designed for this purpose. These may be referred to as macro or micro lenses. Not all close-up photographs require a close-up lens; depending on the size of the evidence, use your best judgment to balance the necessity of capturing detail versus the extra effort involved in changing lenses.
   - The goal is to fill the viewfinder of your camera with the evidence by positioning yourself as close as possible to the evidence while ensuring that the entire item can be captured. This is critical when photographing key items of evidence.
   - Ensure you position the camera at a 90° angle (perpendicular) to the evidence. By avoiding angled shots, you will prevent distortion.
   - Focus your camera very carefully to ensure proper sharpness and clarity of the object. You will probably find that manual focus is often a better option than autofocus when photographing items at close distances.
   - If the item has depth, focus on a midway point (top to bottom) of the evidence; this will help ensure that more of your photographs are sharp and free of blur.
   - Consider the use of a flash or oblique light to ensure proper lighting. Direct flash is often not advised.

- Using a tripod will eliminate blur caused by camera shake that often occurs due to low shutter speeds, which are needed in low-light conditions. A tripod will be necessary for many close-up images. Refer to the specialized photography section of this guide for further information.
- Take at least two images of each item; the first should be without a scale and the second is with a scale. A scale will help provide a size reference. Photographs with scales are absolutely essential for many close-up photographs, especially examination-quality photographs.
- Place scales on the same plan as the key features of the evidence.
- Consider taking additional close-up photographs of items after they have been moved in order to capture details that could not be visualized when the evidence was in its original position at the scene. You must clearly document that these images were taken after the item had been moved, however, in order to avoid later confusion.

4. Saving the images

After completing your photography work at the scene, promptly save your images (uncompressed files, such as TIFF or RAW, are best) in a secure location. This may be a computer, network, or other forms of media. Once your images are saved, then you can make copies of the images which can be disseminated to investigators, prosecutors, defense counsel, etc., if required. We strongly advise that you do not edit, enhance, or otherwise alter any of the original images. This type of work, if necessary, should be completed on the copies and, of course, be thoroughly documented to avoid any suggestion that the original images were altered. Many agencies have specific procedures outlining the process of storing and enhancing images, so be sure to become familiar with your agency requirements.

危機

Chapter 5

Overall Photographs

The first photographs you will generally take to document the crime scene are termed *overall photographs*, referred to by many field practitioners as overalls. The purpose of overall photographs, as their name implies, is to capture the entire (overall) crime scene. These photographs, when properly taken in a methodical and systematic fashion, allow for the creation of a historical visual record of the entire scene, even including areas that did not appear relevant at the time of the examination. Remember that sometimes, the absence of evidence may be just as important as the evidence itself.

Many investigators find it useful to begin the process with a photograph or two that establishes the general location of the crime scene. In most cases this will constitute taking a photograph that reveals the crime scene in conjunction with a nearby reference point. Common reference points may include street intersections, buildings, or any other landmarks which are clearly marked or identifiable. Whenever possible, it is important to choose a permanent reference point since investigators may use these photographs to further analyze various aspects of the scene long after the photographs were actually taken. Keep in mind that these first few establishing photographs may be taken quite a long distance from the actual crime scene.

After you take these establishing photographs, you will follow a methodological approach to photograph the entire crime scene, including outer perimeters and possible entrances and exits used by suspects, victims, or witnesses. If the scene is indoors, you should not limit your photography to indoors, but instead photograph the entire exterior of the structure. Consider to hold your camera whether in the normal horizontal fashion or vertically based on the size and orientation of the subject matter. Narrow, tall objects are usually best photographed using a vertical camera position (Figures 5.1 and 5.2).

Overall Photograph Procedure

Overall photographs must be taken using a methodical process in order to avoid missing any portion of the scene. For indoor scenes, many practitioners prefer to start with exterior photographs, then move inside where the actual crime occurred. This allows for a least-intrusive to most-intrusive approach, thus minimizing potential evidence destruction. Others, however, work from inside to outside, focusing on the primary area first. We have seen both methods used effectively; you will have to make this choice based on the scene itself and your personal preference. What is important is that you follow an organized approach, which will minimize the potential for missing some portion of the scene.

The best method for accomplishing this is to expose a series of slightly overlapping photographs (Figure 5.3). We advise starting at a given point and

(a)

(b)

FIGURE 5.1 These two images depict an entry/exit to a crime scene. As you can see, in both (a) and (b), a standard horizontal camera perspective was used, which prohibited the photographer from capturing the entire doorway in one image.

FIGURE 5.2 This is an image of a door taken with a vertical camera perspective. As you can see, this perspective allows the entire door and frame to be seen.

working either clockwise or counterclockwise until the entire scene is completed. Each photograph should contain a small portion which was present in the previous photograph—hence the term *overlapping*. This overlapping methodology can help later, when investigators use the photographs to analyze the scene. It

FIGURE 5.3 These images depict a series of interior overall images. Notice how the images were taken from a parallel perspective (the photographer positioned himself/herself parallel with the surface being photographed). This helps minimize spatial distortion. Also notice that the photographs are overlapping, which helps to ensure that the entire scene is photographed. *(Continued)*

FIGURE 5.3 (CONTINUED) These images depict a series of interior overall images. Notice how the images were taken from a parallel perspective (the photographer positioned himself/herself parallel with the surface being photographed). This helps minimize spatial distortion. Also notice that the photographs are overlapping, which helps to ensure that the entire scene is photographed. *(Continued)*

FIGURE 5.3 (CONTINUED) These images depict a series of interior overall images. Notice how the images were taken from a parallel perspective (the photographer positioned himself/herself parallel with the surface being photographed). This helps minimize spatial distortion. Also notice that the photographs are overlapping, which helps to ensure that the entire scene is photographed.

will make it easy for the investigator to relate each specific photograph with the overall scene.

To illustrate using an example of a bedroom, one would simply start with a certain wall—the north wall, for instance—then take a series of photographs working around the entire room. If working clockwise from the north wall, one would then photograph the east, south, and west walls, in that order. Of course, if one is working in counter-clockwise fashion the sequence would be reversed. There is no standard number of photographs; you simply take the number that is required to cover that specific area.

In many instances, especially in indoor scenes, the photographer will not be able to photograph the entire height of the walls in one photograph. In these instances, one may choose to take a series of two photographs of a section before moving on to the next section—again, remembering that the photographs should be composed in a slightly overlapping manner. One may choose to work from bottom upward or vice versa, although we recommend using the same method throughout the scene to avoid mistakes and possibly omitting areas. Remember that one may compose hundreds of photographs at a scene, so using a standard and consistent process will automate some of the thought processes, thus reducing chance for error.

Also, do not forget about the floors and ceilings. Since a high volume of evidence is found on floors or the ground, it is always important to photograph the entire floor during the overall photograph process. Depending on the nature and seriousness of the crime, one should consider photographing the ceilings as well. We recommend this especially for crime scenes with blood spatter since impact spatter and cast-off stains are regularly observed on ceilings. Furthermore, the absence of the stains may also be relevant to the investigation.

To avoid distortion, we suggest that you try to avoid diagonal viewpoints when taking your overall photographs. Some have suggested that exposing four photographs from the center of the room is a viable alternative, but we feel that the distortion caused by this type of photograph outweighs any advantages. These diagonal viewpoints will result in some portions of the scene seeming closer in the photograph than they actually are, while other portions will appear further away than they actually are (Figure 5.4). This spatial or perspective distortion could potentially compromise the usefulness of the photographs to investigators or reconstructionists and could cause problems with admissibility in court. Our recommended alternative is to align yourself perpendicular to the portion of the scene you are photographing—so your camera and lens will be parallel with the scene (Figures 5.5 and 5.6). So if you are photographing a wall of an inside crime scene, you would position yourself straight across from the portion of the wall you are capturing. Of course, not every scene will allow this. Some smaller scenes are very difficult to maneuver within, and some scenes will contain evidence or other objects that prohibit proper positioning. In these instances, common sense will prevail: simply position yourself as close as you can to a perpendicular/parallel position—this will reduce the level of distortion. We recommend making a note on the photograph log that the photograph was taken from a diagonal perspective; this will ensure that later viewers are aware of possible distortion problems.

Another factor to be cognizant of is lens choice. Hopefully, you are able to use a zoom lens for your overall photography which will afford you some

(a)

(b)

FIGURE 5.4 These two interior overall images were taken from the center of the room by using a diagonal perspective. Although some crime scene investigators prefer this method, we generally advise against it. As you can see in (a) and (b), spatial distortion is present; the corners of the room appear unusually far away.

FIGURE 5.5 This is an exterior overall image. Notice the parallel perspective.

FIGURE 5.6 Another exterior overall image. Notice that it overlaps with Figure 5.5.

degree of flexibility. Although the use of a normal lens is a great idea, you may find that a wider-angle lens is better suited for small rooms. In small crime scenes, using a normal or telephoto lens will result in each photograph covering only a small portion of the scene, thus causing you to take numerous photographs to capture the area. By using a wide-angle lens, you will be able to cover more area (horizontally), thus reducing the total number of photographs—and thus saving you some time. We advise against using extreme wide-angle lens since this may cause bending at the outer edges of the photographs called barrel distortion, but allowing yourself the flexibility of using a wider than normal range will, again, allow you to capture more area without significantly altering the perspective of the scene.

An example: To illustrate the overall photography process, let us use an example of a homicide committed within the kitchen of a two-story residence. You would begin by establishing the location of the residence; maybe an intersection a half-block away. You would photograph the intersection street signs with the crime scene residence in the background. Then you may move to the exterior of the residence and photograph the structure, and curtilage, in a 360° fashion—all the way around the house. Once complete, you would move into the interior of the home and photograph each and every room, hallway, closet, or any other space using the aforementioned methodical process. You would also consider photographing any pathways that may have been used by the suspect or victim. After this process is complete, the overall sequence is finished and you would begin to focus on photographing specific items of evidence.

So that is it; in a nutshell, overall photographs serve to document the entire crime scene. As you can see, it is critical that all portions of the scene, to include possible pathways used by victims or suspects, be captured. By using a methodical, overlapping, method you will be less likely to miss any portion of the scene.

危機

Chapter 6

Mid-Range Photographs

Mid-range photographs, along with sketching, should accurately depict items of evidence, and their spatial relationships, within the scene. Mid-range photographs must be portrayed accurately and without distortion in order to achieve this purpose. They should allow viewers to visualize the specific locations of the evidence in proper context; that is, the location of the evidence should be viewable in a manner which accurately depicts the location in relation to key objects or fixtures within the scene (see Figure 6.1a and b). Unfortunately, this is one area that is often overlooked. Beware—many novice crime scene photographers simply take photographs of evidence from several feet away, assuming these meet the requirements of mid-range photography. This may result in inaccurate distance depictions of evidence (see Figures 6.2 through 6.4) when viewed within the context of other items at the crime scene. By following the advice presented in this guide, you can be sure to avoid this common pitfall.

Generally, crime scene photographers expose mid-range photographs after overall photographs and before close-up photographs are taken. This sequence follows

(a)

(b)

FIGURE 6.1 These are mid-range images depicting a knife and blood in relation to a fixed feature, in this case, the corner of stairs. Notice how the photographer formed an isosceles triangle, ensured he/she was at an equal distance from both the evidence and the fixed feature. Note that the photographer took photographs from different distances, closer to the evidence and fixed feature in (a) and further away from the evidence and fixed feature in (b), but still maintained a proper perspective by ensuring that he/she was at an equal distance from the evidence and fixed feature.

FIGURE 6.2 Contrast this improperly composed mid-range image with the images in Figure 6.1a and b. Notice how the distance between the evidence and the reference point is distorted (appears closer than it actually was).

a standard least-intrusive to most-intrusive progression which, when combined with other proper crime scene protocols, allows investigators to avoid unintentional destruction or contamination of evidence.

The following technique combines several elements which can be used to ensure that mid-range photographs are of sufficient quality and achieve their intended purpose. First, it is important to consider the composition of the photograph. In most instances, when possible, a natural perspective should be used, meaning that the viewer of the image should be able to see essentially what you, the photographer, observed at the scene. Of course, items under furniture or in other unusual locations will require flexibility inthe application of this natural perspective. Also, a photographer may wish to alter the perspective in order to eliminate distracting objects. This decision

(a)

(b)

FIGURE 6.3 These images demonstrate the idea that mid-range photographs help establish the relationship between different items of evidence within the scene. (a) This image, in concert with b, helps the viewer to understand the layout of the scene in relation to various items of evidence. (b) The location of the bloodstains in this image in relation to other items in the scene can be established with this image in conjunction with a.

(*Continued*)

(c)

FIGURE 6.3 (CONTINUED) These images demonstrate the idea that mid-range photographs help establish the relationship between different items of evidence within the scene. (c) This image demonstrates the spatial relationship between the mask and the knife. This image, in addition to overall images, allows the viewer to clearly understand the precise location of these two items in relation to each other and other items in the room.

must be based on logic, experience, and a strong awareness of all aspects of the photograph—the foreground, the background, and its sides.

Mid-range photographs are composed of an item of evidence (or other important object) in conjunction with a fixed object or other key items which serve as a reference point. For example, the location of a cartridge case in relation to a deceased victim would be highly relevant. So it would be worthwhile to take mid-range photographs to establish the relationship of the cartridge case not only to a fixed feature (such as a corner in the room), but also to the body. So, with this in mind, you can see that, depending on the circumstances and nature of the scene, several mid-range

FIGURE 6.4 This image is an example showing how spatial distortion can occur if the photographer does not maintain proper positioning. In this case, instead of forming an isosceles triangle, the photographer arranged the evidence (hammer) and fixed feature in a straight line. The result is a condensed or elongated appearance of items beyond the evidence. You can see that the tiles in the back of the image appear smaller and more condensed even though they are the same size throughout. You can also help minimize this by zooming in to eliminate the presence of background items.

photographs from a variety of positions may be necessary to thoroughly document the location and spatial relationships of a single item of evidence.

Photographer positioning: Although there are usually a number of perspectives from which the evidence and reference point can be photographed, there are some general rules which must be followed to ensure that the spatial relationships are in proper proportion and provide an accurate representation. In order to achieve the perspective that most accurately represents the scene, you should position yourself an equal distance from both the evidence and the reference point. The idea is to form an isosceles triangle, with the photographer at one vertex positioned an equal distance from both the evidence and the reference point. The photographer may be positioned at various locations, as long as he/she is an approximate equal distance from both the evidence and fixed object/reference point. Properly choosing this position may depend upon a couple of factors. First, the scene itself may limit the photographer to a single position since obstructions such as furniture, walls, or other evidence may limit movement. Second, the photographer may find that being further away, or closer, to the evidence and fixed object/reference point provides a more useful image. As mentioned earlier, we thoroughly recommend that the photographer take mid-range photographs of key items of evidence from a variety of vantage points while being mindful of the positioning guidelines. You may also consider use of placards to help draw attention to the evidence (see Figures 6.5 and 6.6).

Focusing: To avoid distortion, we recommend that you focus on an area halfway between the evidence and the fixed object/reference point. The evidence should be on one side of the viewfinder, and the fixed object/reference point should be on the opposite side. Many novice crime scene photographers tend to focus solely on the evidence, a practice that may result in spatial distortion, meaning that an accurate distance between the evidence and reference point cannot be

FIGURE 6.5 This is a mid-range image without placards. Compare this with the image in Figure 6.6; you can see how the use of placards can help draw attention to items of evidence. You would also take mid-range images from a closer distance, but still maintaining the isosceles triangle perspective.

determined. This could potentially render the image inadmissible in court and useless to later investigative activity.

Lens choice is a very important factor contributing to the quality of mid-range photographs. A normal lens allows the image to appear most similar to that which would be observed by one's eyes (without a camera). For a 35 mm single-lens reflex film camera, the normal lens is a 50 mm lens. Digital cameras, however, have differently sized sensors, which results in the variation from the standard 50 mm lens being considered normal. Many moderately priced cameras

FIGURE 6.6 This image reveals how the use of placards may help bring attention to the evidence. Without the placards, the evidence may be inconspicuous. If you use placards, make sure to photograph the evidence in situ (as it was) prior to placement of placards.

have smaller sensors, resulting in the normal lens being somewhere in the vicinity of 30–40 mm. Because of this, the use of a 50 mm lens would result in the photograph appearing magnified, or cropped. It would be wise for any crime scene photographer to become familiar with normal lens lengths for his/her camera. To determine the normal lens length for your camera, you may consult your camera guide, contact the manufacturer, or consult online camera specifications through the manufacturer website.

There will be times when the use of a normal lens is not practical. Barriers, such as furniture or other evidence, may prevent you from positioning yourself in a manner that would allow you to use a normal lens (remember that the evidence should be on one side of the viewfinder with the reference point on the opposite side). So you may have to move closer or further away. By zooming your lens, you will be able to magnify or elongate your scene. So long as you maintain the proper perspective of having the evidence and reference point on opposite sides of the viewfinder, this will not be problematic—so long as the background and foreground is minimized.

Hopefully, this section will allow you to quickly and accurately photograph your scene in a method which ensures the accuracy of spatial relationships. Remember a few key tips: position yourself at an equal distance from the evidence and reference point and ensure the evidence and reference point are located at opposite ends of the camera's viewfinder. By following this method, you can establish generally accurate spatial relationships between any two items at a crime scene.

危機

CHAPTER 7

Close-Up Photographs

The final step in photographing evidence is a series of close-ups which, as the name implies, will require you to position the camera in close proximity to physical evidence (see Figure 7.1). The objective is to visually record the fine details of the evidence. The relevancy and usefulness of these close-ups will ultimately be determined by the evidence itself and the circumstances of the case. In virtually all instances, however, close-ups will serve to record the specific conditions of the item of evidence, identifying features (such as vehicle identification numbers and serial numbers) and, if taken properly, the size of the item (see Figures 7.2 through 7.9).

You should be aware of an important distinction between standard items of evidence and evidence which may be compared to other items in a crime laboratory. The latter category will require you to take very specific steps to ensure that forensic scientists are able to use your photographs to make comparisons. Common forms of comparison evidence include bite marks, fingerprints, shoe impressions/prints, and tire impressions/prints. These types of close up photographs are often referred to as examination-quality

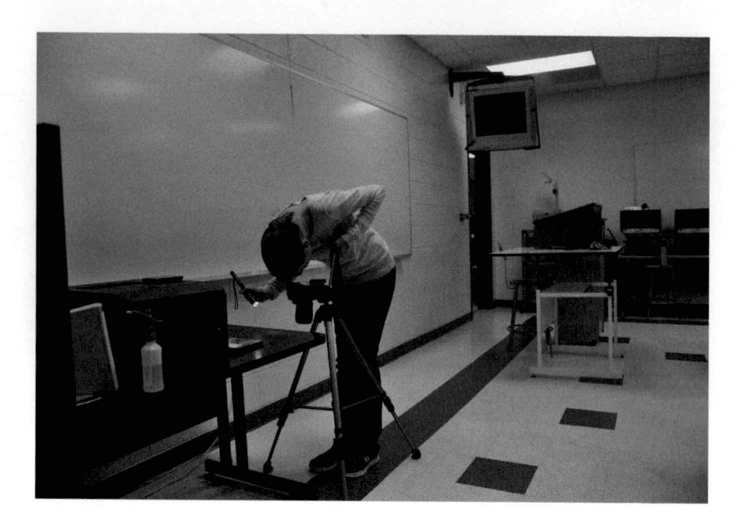

FIGURE 7.1 This image shows a person composing a close-up image of evidence. Notice how the camera body is in a parallel position with the surface on which the evidence is located. The camera is positioned as close as possible to the evidence in order to fill the frame with the evidence. In this instance, the photographer is using oblique white light to help visualize the evidence. A tripod is used to prevent blur from camera shake, which will occur when slow shutter speeds are used.

photographs. Mistakes in photography may render forensic examinations impossible; thus, precision and accuracy is required. For this reason, we have provided step-by-step instructions for many of these types of evidence within subsequent sections of the guide.

Steps

Close-up photographs are generally taken of an item of evidence immediately after mid-range shots. Some of these close-up shots will require changing the lens since most zoom lenses used in crime scene photography will not allow you to position yourself close

FIGURE 7.2 This is a close-up image of a cartridge case. Filling the frame allows easy visualization of key details.

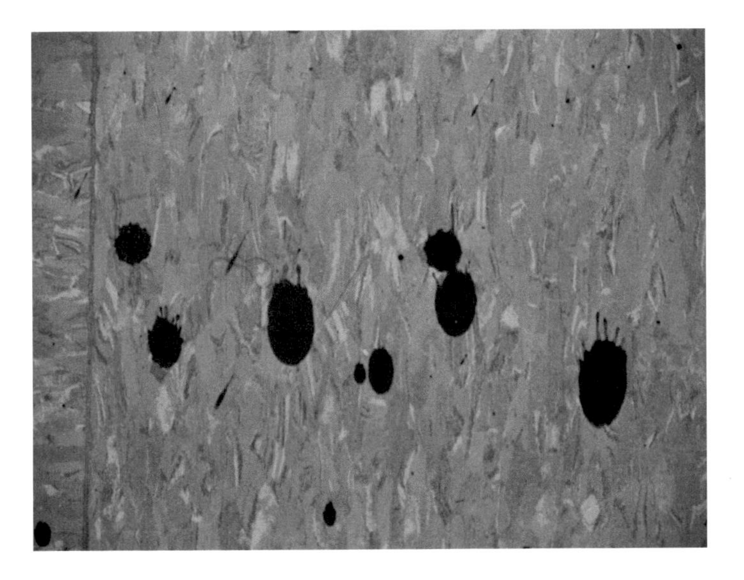

FIGURE 7.3 This image depicts bloodstain evidence without a scale.

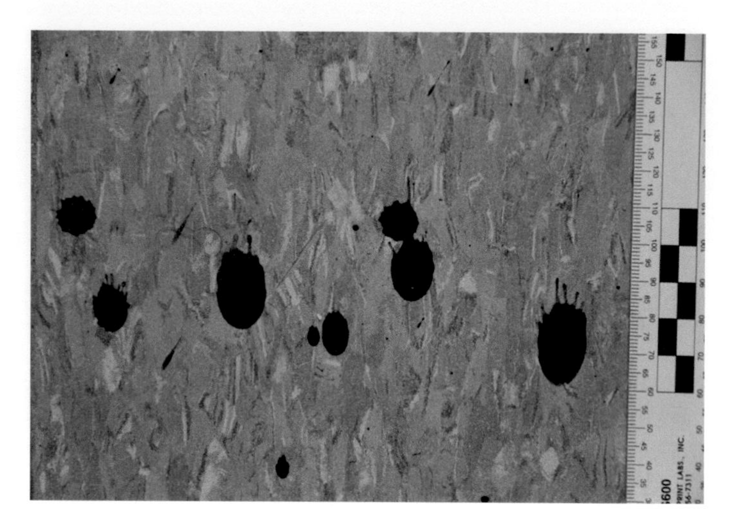

FIGURE 7.4 This is the same bloodstain as in Figure 7.3, but with a scale.

FIGURE 7.5 This is an L-shaped scale commonly used for footwear print and impression evidence.

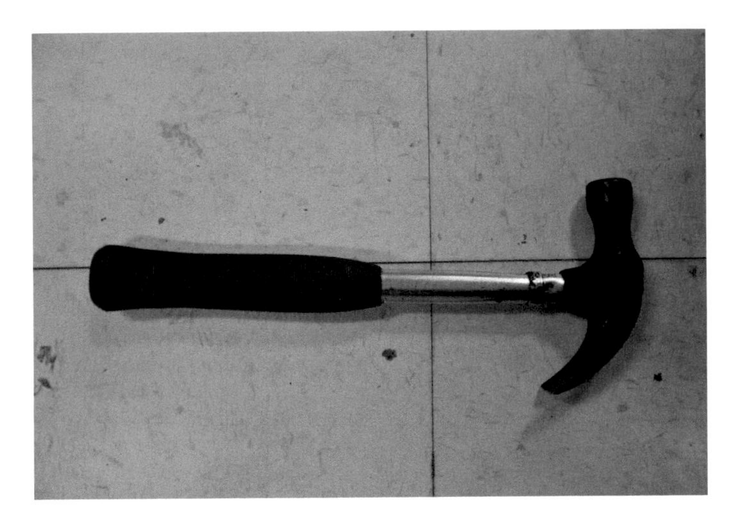

FIGURE 7.6 This image is a close-up of a hammer. Because of the size of the hammer, a macro lens was not necessary. Additional photographs from closer range may be necessary if trace evidence is present.

enough to small items of evidence necessary to capture the fine details of the item. Lens manufacturers produce lenses specifically designed for close-up photography, and we strongly advise that you use these for some of your close-up work.

Close-up photographs of any item of evidence, or other relevant objects, will require at least two photographs, sometimes more. The first in the sequence will be without the use of a scale. The item will be photographed as it is, in its unaltered state. After this unaltered photograph, you should place a scale (we recommend an L-shaped scale available through many forensic supply distributors) near the item so the size of the item is properly recorded. Scaled photographs are especially important for items of evidence which cannot maintain their shape and size—such as a bloodstain on a floor.

FIGURE 7.7 This is a close-up image of a partial footwear dust impression, visualized with white, oblique light.

In many instances, the sole long-term record of the bloodstains size will be your notes and photographs. In addition, it is critical to use a scale for any examination-quality photograph. When placing your scale near the evidence, be sure that you place it parallel with the key features. This may require a bit of effort for footwear or tire impressions, since the ridge features may be a few or even several inches below the top surface of the impression. Figure 7.10 depicts several common scales used in crime scene photography.

Additional close-ups may be required if you wish to record certain aspects of the evidence that were not photographed prior to the item being moved. Some prefer to take these photographs in a controlled

FIGURE 7.8 This image is a close-up of a fingerprint.

environment, for example, within an evidence processing area, rather than at the crime scene, to avoid possible confusion regarding how the evidence was actually positioned within the scene prior to it being moved (see Figures 7.11 through 7.13). If you do choose to take close-up photographs of a moved item at the scene, you must specifically document this in your photograph log. This documentation would, of course, serve as reference for investigators or in court should questions arise.

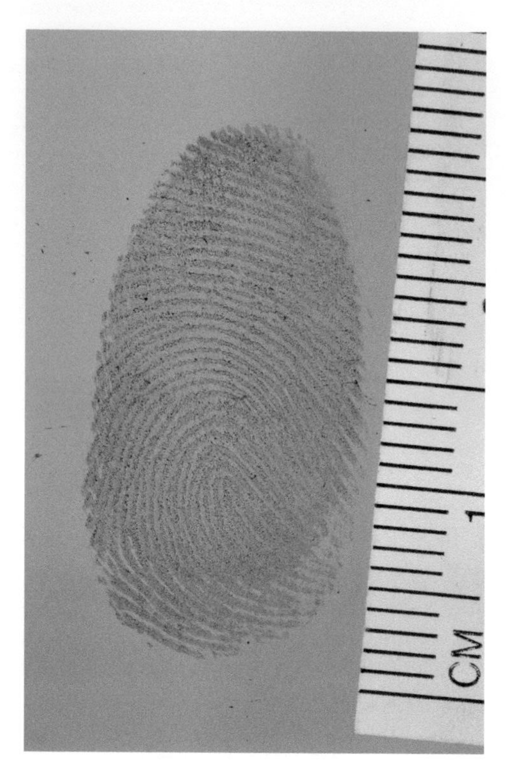

FIGURE 7.9 This is another image of a fingerprint; notice how the print fills the frame. Such a view will require you to position your camera very close to the print.

Close-Up Photograph Tips

Make sure the item you are photographing fills the entire viewfinder of your camera or as much as is practical given the lens and the environment. Do not cut any portion of the evidence out of the photograph, but do not waste space either. This is often referred to as "filling the frame," a phrase used in relation to film

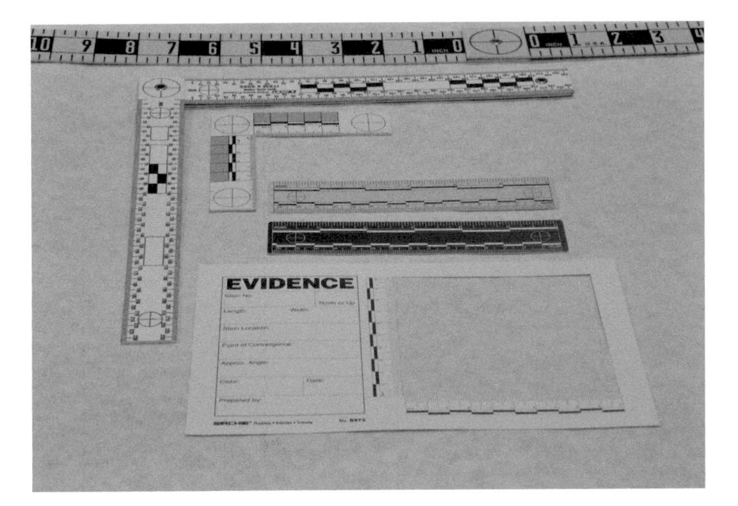

FIGURE 7.10 This image depicts various types of scales that can be used during the close-up photography sequence.

FIGURE 7.11 This image is a close-up of a boot found as is at a crime scene.

FIGURE 7.12 This is an altered close-up of the same boot depicted in Figure 7.11. It is important to document in your log that the evidence was altered prior to the images being taken. This could prevent future confusion, possibly months or years later, in the courtroom.

FIGURE 7.13 This is an altered close-up of the same boot depicted in Figure 7.11.

cameras, with the frame representing the area of the photograph. Close positioning will reduce or prevent the requirement to digitally zoom in on the evidence to view fine details. This digital zooming process results in a loss of clarity, so avoiding it to the extent possible is advised. This will require you to position the camera, often using a tripod, extremely close to the item, especially when dealing with small items such as fingerprints, fibers, and so on. You should orient your camera in a manner which is best able to fill the viewfinder with the evidence (see Figure 7.14). So, for example, if you are photographing a hammer positioned with its length oriented north to south, you should position your camera so the length of the hammer extends width-wise across your viewfinder since this will allow you to move as close as possible to the evidence. Every lens has a minimum focusing distance, and it is wise to understand where your lens limits are for your camera.

You should consider using a tripod to reduce camera shake. A tripod will allow you to photograph items when insufficient lighting is available and help keep the camera in proper position. As you will see in subsequent sections, the use of oblique light techniques is often helpful, or essential, in capturing key details of impression evidence. Tripods should always be used in these instances.

The use of flash can substitute for inadequate lighting, but may pose challenges, primarily hotspots caused by direct flashes. If you find that your close-up photographs contain these hotspots, then you have a few options. First, you may consider using a tripod and simply refraining from using the flash; this will potentially require adjustments to the exposure settings. Another option may be to turn your flash unit

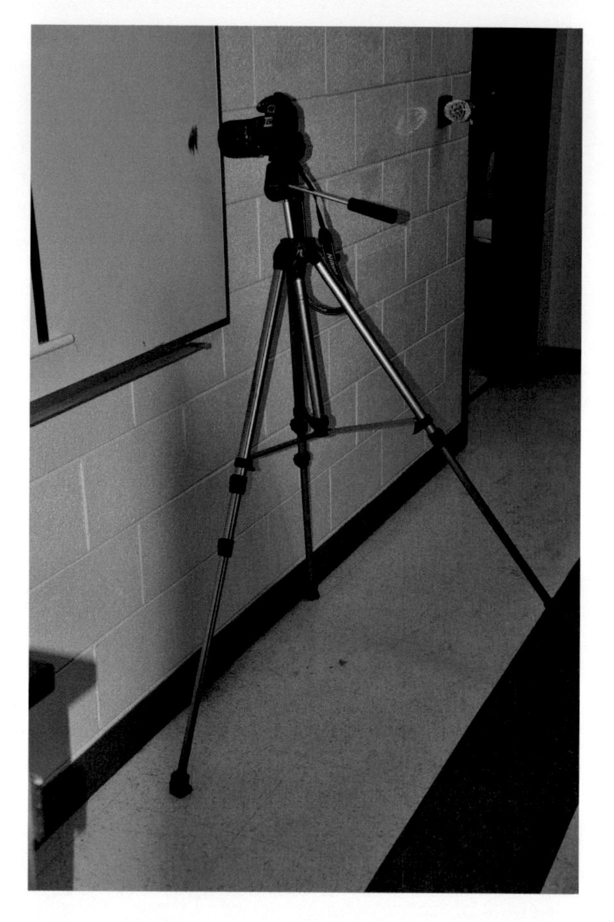

FIGURE 7.14 This image depicts the position of the tripod used to capture a fingerprint. Notice the camera is positioned along the long axis of the print in order to fill the frame.

so it does not directly strike the item you are photographing. You can use the bounce light technique described in Chapter 3. Finally, you may soften the flash by using one of the methods also described in Chapter 3. The decision of which method to employ will ultimately rest with your preferences and the scene conditions.

When photographing objects with depth, such as a footwear impression in dirt, it may be difficult to achieve a clear focus on all aspects of the object. One common problem is that the specific point of focus will be clear, but the other portion of the object will be out of focus. So if you were to focus on the top portion of the ridges of a shoe impression, the bottom portion of the ridges may be out of focus. This is a depth of field problem. Here are a couple of tips to help avoid this and help ensure that all relevant portions of your photograph are in focus. First, avoid using wide apertures (low f-stop numbers). Anything below an f-8 will likely result in a poor depth of field—so keep the tripod handy since using a small aperture (high f-stop) will possibly result in insufficient lighting. Second, instead of focusing on the top or bottom of the item, focus in the middle. This will also help ensure the entire portion of the image is in focus.

When you take close-up photographs, hold your camera in a manner which allows the lens of the camera to be parallel with the item you are photographing. By ensuring this parallel perspective, you will avoid your evidence appearing distorted in the photograph. Of course, distortion of evidence may hinder forensic examinations, present an unrealistic appearance to investigators who may examine the photographs at a later juncture, and possibly preclude the images from being admitted into court.

危機

Chapter 8

Photographing Footwear/ Tire Tracks and Impressions

Indoor Dust Impressions

Like latent prints, footwear and tire-wear impressions need special attention when photographing them in a crime scene. Footwear impressions represent the single most often overlooked type of evidence. A suspect may wear gloves or not leave any DNA in a scene, but he/she has to walk in the scene. Depending on the surface, there are usually impressions left by his/her shoes. In most cases, it is just a question of using effective search methods. Even if the initial response to the scene involved multiple first responders walking throughout the scene, it is always worth a look. The best way to search for these impressions on floors is through the use of oblique light. Using a bright flashlight, simply place the light so the beam skims the surface of the floor (see

Figure 8.1). This oblique light, even on light-colored floors, will allow impressions left in the dust on the floor to stand out. And if you can see them, you can photograph them. Darker scenes make this process easier, but even in brighter scenes, it is possible to get a good quality image.

Photographing a footwear impression on a dusty floor requires a DSLR camera, a flash with a sync cord or a flashlight, a scale, and a tripod. After taking the appropriate sequence of overall and mid-range photographs with and without placards, next comes the

FIGURE 8.1 This photograph depicts the setup for using a flashlight to take two-dimensional footwear impressions. Note that the camera is on a tripod, and a scale is placed on the floor. The flashlight is then used at an oblique angle at various positions around the footwear impression to bring out the impression from the background.

task of taking a close-up of the impression. The following is a step-by-step sequence:

- Place the camera on a tripod with the back of the camera parallel to the floor.
- Compose the image in the viewfinder. You should fill the frame making sure your scale is also part of the image. Preferably, the scale should extend the entire length of the impression. Some forensic supply distributors sell long L-shaped scales that are perfect for footwear impressions.
- After scale placement, it often helps to light the impression with your flashlight to see it as you compose the image; this also helps in focusing if the lighting is dark. If the room is brightly lit, darkening the room may help to see the impression as well.
- Set your camera to the lowest ISO available and make sure that you use an uncompressed file format (RAW or TIFF).
- Place the camera in manual exposure mode. Set the aperture to f-11 and adjust your shutter speed so as to underexpose the image by a full stop.
- Set your flash mode to manual and dial down the flash output to its halfway point.
- Take the photograph.
- Depending on the amount of light in the room, your image may be overexposed or underexposed. Adjust your flash output accordingly, making sure to keep the flash to impression distance consistent. You will find that you probably achieve the best results by placing the flash about two feet away from the beginning of the

impression. Any closer and the fall off from the flash will not illuminate the entire length of the impression.

Another method, using a flashlight, is perhaps a bit faster. Instead of using a flash, simply illuminate the impression with your flashlight held at a very oblique angle (just above the floor). You will likely find that holding the flashlight up to five or six feet away from the impression will yield the best results. Set up the camera with similar settings, but instead of configuring the camera up to underexpose, dial the shutter speed up or down to the point where the image is properly exposed according to the camera's metering system. Take the photograph. Depending on the lighting conditions and the color of the floor, you may need to adjust the shutter speed to add or remove light to ensure that there is sufficient contrast in the photograph to see the entire impression. Illuminating the impression with a flashlight can also be used when taking a footwear impression with a point-and-shoot type of camera. Again, using a tripod, place the camera over the impression with the back of the camera parallel to the surface. If the camera has a manual mode, set the camera up with similar settings to those used with a DSLR camera. If an uncompressed file format is not available on your camera, select the largest compressed format available.

Take the photograph and adjust the settings as necessary to achieve sufficient contrast to see the entire impression. If the point-and-shoot camera has no manual mode, you may still be able to capture the image by turning the flash off and lighting the impression with a flashlight and allowing the camera to determine the appropriate settings. You must remember, however, that the camera must be on a tripod. This allows the camera to use very slow shutter speeds by keeping the camera very still during the exposure.

Photographing Prints Lifted with an Electrostatic Dust Print Lifter

Crime scene investigators regularly employ electrostatic dust print lifters (ESDLs) to lift dust impressions. We have found it useful to obtain additional photographs of the dust impression after the image has been lifted with the ESDL (see Figures 8.2 and 8.3), just in case the impression becomes destroyed prior to reaching the forensic laboratory. The technique is very similar to photographing the dust

FIGURE 8.2 This photograph demonstrates what the two-dimensional footwear impression looks like when taken with a flashlight as a light source.

FIGURE 8.3 This photograph shows the same footwear impression after being lifted using ESDL and using a detached flash as a light source.

impressions prior to them being lifted by the ESDL. Here are the steps:

- Affix the ESDL lift to a wall using tape.
- Affix a scale to the lift. You may use an adhesive scale or tape a regular scale.
- Set your camera on a tripod. Make sure that the back of the camera is parallel to the ESDL lift.
- Fill the viewfinder with the impression, making sure to include the scale.
- Set the exposure mode to manual. Select f-11 and a shutter speed of six seconds. Place your ISO on 100 or lower.
- Illuminate the impression using a flashlight, held at a very oblique angle, about two to three feet away from the impression.
- Depress the shutter and pan the light *evenly* over the entire impression. Make sure to move the entire flashlight; do not just pivot it from one

position. Pivoting it would result in an overexposed portion of the impression near the light source.

- Review the image and adjust the shutter speed to either increase or decrease exposure.

Outdoor Photography of Impressions

Like indoor impressions, outdoor impressions will also require a tripod and oblique light (see Figure 8.4). After taking the necessary overall and mid-range images, you are now ready to take the close-up photographs. However, there is a new wrinkle in an outdoor impression. Many of the impressions outdoors are going to be three dimensional, meaning there will be some depth to the impression (Figure 8.5). You will need to take this into account when placing your scale.

FIGURE 8.4 This photograph demonstrates the setup for taking footwear impressions in three dimensions outdoors.

FIGURE 8.5 This photograph shows a trail of footwear impressions in snow.

Unlike a footwear impression on a floor, which is essentially a two-dimensional impression, impressions which have depth are subject to perspective distortion. What that means is the scale you place in the photograph must be at the same depth as the bottom of the impression, not at the top. To do this, simply dig a slight depression to the same depth as the impression in the area next to the impression so the entire scale can rest at the bottom of the depression. As you dig the depression, be very careful to not disturb the impression (Figures 8.6 and 8.7).

The ambient light is another factor which must be considered. On an overcast day, controlling the lighting conditions is straightforward; you can rely on your metering system. On a bright, sunny day, however, it can be quite difficult. Since the objective is to create contrast in order to enhance the visibility of the small details at the bottom of the impression,

FIGURE 8.6 This image is a close-up of three-dimensional impressions in sand and snow.

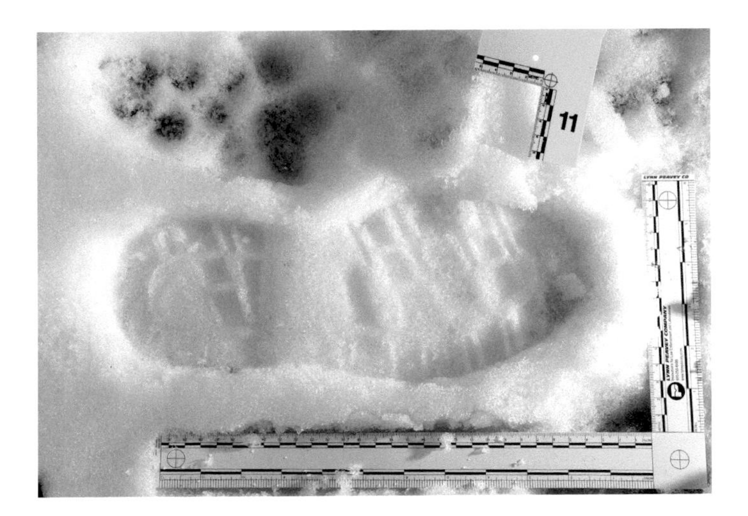

FIGURE 8.7 This is another image of three-dimensional impressions in sand and snow.

you will need to have it dark enough for the flash to do the job. But on a bright day, unless you can shade the impression, the flash is simply not powerful enough to create the necessary contrast. This is going to be even more problematic if you are using a flashlight in lieu of a flash unit. Because of this, if the impression is in full sun, you will need to shade it. There is no other alternative. You can shade the impression by using a blanket, cardboard box, etc., anything that will block the direct rays of the sun. We have found that using black paper is an effective method. Rolls of black paper are available through forensic distributors. Blocking the light from two sides is best simply because you are creating a deeper shade. Once the scale is in place (remember to place it as the same depth as the bottom of the impression) and the impression is shaded, you are ready to set up the camera. Here are the steps:

- Set the camera on a tripod. Make sure that the back of the camera is parallel to the impression. Particular attention must be paid if the impression is located on an incline. You will need to adjust your tripod accordingly in order to maintain a 90° angle between the back of your camera and the impression.
- Next, compose the impression in your viewfinder, making sure to fill the frame.
- Connect the flash unit to the camera using a sync cord. You will be required to hold the flash in at least three different positions around the impression, so the sync cord is a necessity.
- Place the camera on manual exposure mode. Set your f-stop to f-11 and your ISO to the lowest available for your camera. Now adjust your

shutter speed to underexpose the image by a full exposure value.

- Hold the flash so it fires at an approximately 45° angle toward the impression from a distance of about four or five feet away from the impression.
- Take some test exposures. Evaluate the exposure and adjust the shutter speed and flash output as needed to achieve contrast between the shadows and illuminated parts of the impression. Adjust the angle of the flash to allow it to create shadows from the elevated parts of the impression while still getting light into the bottom of the impression. Once you achieve a proper exposure, take two additional images bracketing the exposure with a +1 and –1.
- Next, move the flash to take a sequence of photographs from different positions around the impression so the shadows it creates are different in each photograph. A good rule of thumb is to position the flash so the light travels between each of the tripod legs. This will remind you to take several photographs with the flash at different positions. Another method that might help you understand this process is imagining a circle around the impression. The circle would be about 10 feet in diameter. You will hold the flash at three positions around the circle's circumference. The flash positions should be about equidistant from each other. Remember that you have to keep the flash to impression distance and the angle of the flash consistent to make sure your exposure does not change. Bracketing your exposures is also recommended. By bracketing +1 and –1 exposure values, you will have some latitude for error in exposure. After all is said and

done, you should have taken at least nine images of the footwear impression—three from each of the different flash positions.

Tire Impressions

Tire impressions are going to be photographed in a similar manner (see Figures 8.8 and 8.9). The equipment setup and the exposure processes are going to be the same. Likewise, you will need to shade the impression and place your scale at the same depth as the impression. Where tire impressions differ, you will need to take the sequence around the tripod several times along the length of the impression. This is done to ensure that you capture the full circumference of the tire. The circumference of a tire can vary from six to over eight feet or more depending on the tire. A

FIGURE 8.8 This is a mid-range image of three-dimensional tire-wear impressions in snow.

FIGURE 8.9 This is another mid-range image of three-dimensional tire-wear impressions in snow.

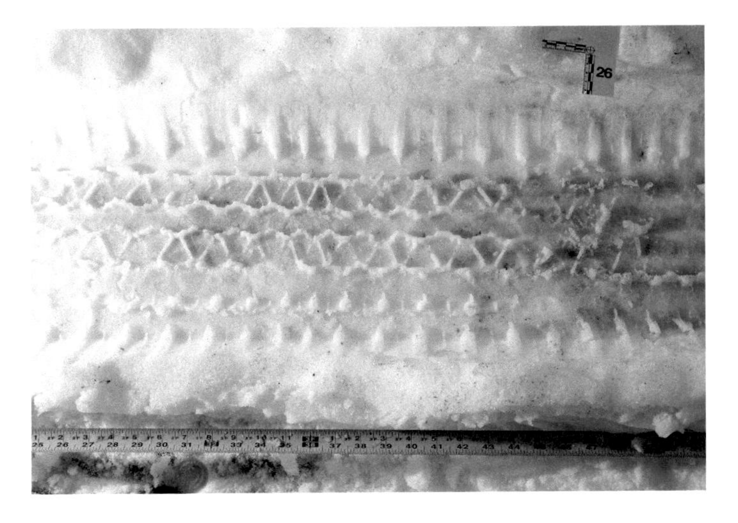

FIGURE 8.10 Using the same setup as shown in Figure 8.4, this is a close-up of part of the tire-wear impression in snow.

good rule of thumb is to photograph at least eight feet of the impression, in one-foot sections. If you have evidence to suggest that the tire is larger than a standard tire, photographing more than eight feet may be called for. But if you do the math on an eight-foot section of an impression at one-foot intervals, with at least three photographs per section, well, you are talking about 24 total photographs. And if you bracket, which you should if there is any doubt about whether the exposure is correct, you could easily end up with nearly 75 photographs of the tire impression. This can be a lot of work! (Figure 8.10).

Chapter 9

Photographing Latent Fingerprints

So, you have found a latent print in your scene. It may seem unnecessary to photograph latent prints once they have been developed. After all, you are just going to lift the print after you develop it, right? Well, maybe. Depending on the surface, the lift may not come off the way you expect. It is fairly common for a latent print to look fabulous when you apply the powder, but look like a black smudge after you lift it and place it on the card. That is why it is always a good idea to photograph the print before any attempt to lift it. Having a good photograph of the print is a bit like having a backup gun; you may not need it, but it is nice to have in case your primary gun malfunctions.

There are a few things to recall from previous chapters. First, fill the frame with the print. To do so, you will orient the camera to align with the long axis of the print. That is usually a fairly easy thing to do with a single fingerprint. However, palm prints, especially if it is a full palm, may be roughly square in overall shape. Or you may encounter a series of two, three, or four fingerprints deposited simultaneously. In that case, fill the frame the best you can in a manner which allows the best visualization of the entire print or prints. Do not forget to include a scale as part of your image. We find that the addition of an adhesive scale is handy since you can avoid the difficulty of holding a regular scale in place while simultaneously operating the camera. You can also write on the adhesive scale to keep track of which print is which when you have a multitude of latent prints in a scene.

Second, get as close to the surface on which the print is located as your camera and lens will allow. Your camera and lens have a minimum focus distance, and it varies with each camera/lens combination. Inside the minimum focus distance, you will not be able to focus the image. We strongly recommend using a macro lens to allow getting as close to the surface as possible.

Third, remember that the depth of field is very shallow when photographing an object up close. That means that even the tiniest amount of back-and-forth movement can cause an out-of-focus photograph. For that reason, we recommend placing the camera on a tripod. By doing so, you allow the camera to focus on the surface from a fixed distance. Hand-holding the camera increases the possibility of taking an out-of-focus photograph due to body movement.

The ideal equipment for photographing a latent print consists of a tripod, flash, remote (sync) cord for the flash, DSLR camera, and macro lens. If your department does not possess these items, we will prescribe some alternatives.

Photographing a Latent Print: Step by Step

- Place the camera on the tripod securely.
- Set the camera to take an uncompressed image, a TIFF or RAW image if that setting is available on your camera.
- Set the camera on aperture priority mode and set your aperture to f-11. Use a low ISO setting; 100 is probably going to achieve the best result.
- Before attaching the flash, compose the photograph to make sure that the camera can focus on the print and ensure that the print (and the scale) fills the image frame. If necessary, adjust the camera position to allow the camera to focus and fill the frame. Also, remember to keep the sensor plane parallel to the surface to minimize perspective distortion.
- Attach the sync cord to the flash and camera. Position the flash head so it is aimed at the print. Take the picture. Ideally, you have a well-exposed and well-composed photograph of the print.
- An alternative method to using flash is the utilization of a flashlight. Aim the flashlight at an oblique angle at the latent print. You may find that moving the flashlight 360° around the print while maintaining the oblique angle will allow you to find a specific direction that will provide for the best visualization of the print. Once this position is determined, take the photograph. You can adjust exposure in the same manner as you would with flash, using the exposure compensation function.
- Using the image viewer on the camera, zoom into the image and take a look to see if you have

captured the small details of the print. You should be able to clearly see small details in the print. Depending on the clarity of the print, you may be able to see individual pores along the ridges. You should be able to see surface variations. If you have that kind of detail in the image, your focus was most likely spot on. If those details are there but a bit unclear, you may have been a bit off with the focus. Also, review the exposure. Any white parts of the image should be white; black parts of the image should be black. If the image is over- or underexposed, you should take another photograph and adjust the exposure settings appropriately using the exposure compensation feature on your camera.

These aforementioned steps are for setup for indoor photography. Indoor lighting is, for the most part, pretty stable. In brightly lit scenes or very dark scenes, you will need to adjust your settings accordingly. Also, outdoor lighting commonly has high contrast. You can be working inside a car and have somewhat dim lighting, and then move to photograph a print on the exterior and be in a very bright environment. Outdoors, you have to be on your toes and adjust your settings as frequently as the lighting conditions change.

But what if you do not have a DSLR camera, external flash, or a tripod? You can still get a quality photograph of the print; it is just going to be a bit more difficult. With a point-and-shoot-type camera, a zoom lens, and a built in flash, you have to learn to work around the limitations of your equipment. Your point and shoot camera will attach to a tripod, so if one is available, we recommend using it. Absent a tripod, use your arms, elbows, etc., to brace yourself in such a way as to minimize movement. Remember that your minimum focus distance will limit how close you can position the camera in relation to the print. The built-in flash will not work in this case, so turn it off. Set the camera to aperture mode if it has one. Set the aperture to the middle of the aperture range. Set your ISO to 400 or 800 to allow for a faster exposure and to minimize camera shake. Set the camera to take an uncompressed image if that option is available. If not, use the largest file size setting available. We want to capture as large an image file as possible.

Using an external light source like a flashlight, light up the latent print (it is easiest to do this with a partner). Zoom in using the zoom lens and fill the frame to the maximum extent allowed by your camera and minimum focus distance. Take the photograph.

Using the image viewer on the camera, zoom into the image and determine if you have captured the small details of the print. You should be able to clearly see small details in the print. Depending on the clarity of the print, you may be able to see individual pores along the ridges. You should be able to see surface variations. If you have that kind of detail in the image, your focus was most likely spot on. If those details are there but a bit unclear, you may have been a bit off with the focus. Take a look at the exposure. Any white parts of the image should be white; black parts of the image should be black. If the image is over- or underexposed, you should take another photograph and move the flashlight closer or farther away to add more or less light depending on what you need. Figures 9.1 through 9.3 are photographs of latent prints developed at crime scenes.

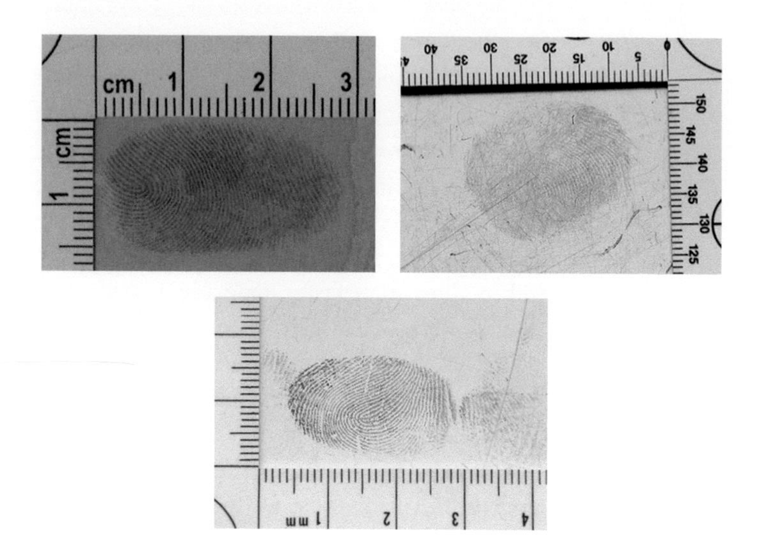

FIGURE 9.1 These images are close-ups of single digit latent prints. Note that in each case, the scale is visible and the frame is filled to capture the most amount of detail possible.

Regardless of which type of camera you are using, we recommend taking several photographs of the print. This helps increase your chances that at least one or two of the images will be properly focused and properly exposed. As with any close-up photograph, you should have several overall and mid-range photographs of the latent before you start taking your close-up photographs. As we mentioned in our earlier chapters, you need the overall and mid-range photographs to help put the close-up into its proper context.

Remember that the settings we described here are well suited for your average indoor scene. If your scene is very bright or very dark, you will need to adjust your settings to suit the lighting conditions. This is particularly true if you are working outdoors, especially on a bright, sunny day.

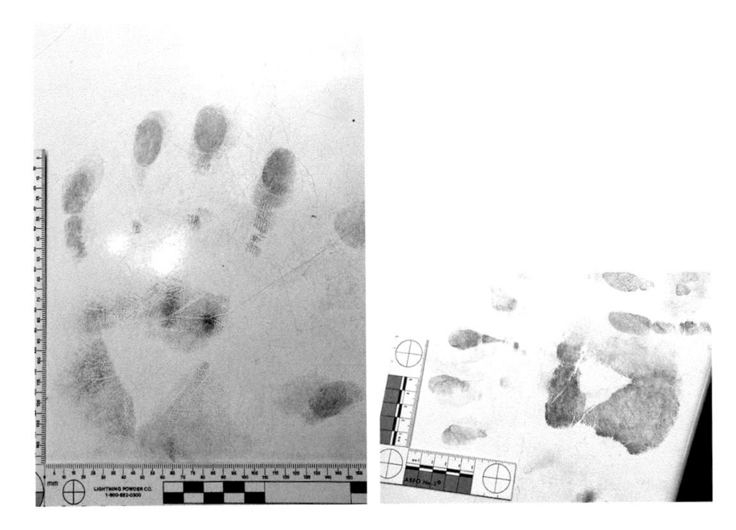

FIGURE 9.2 These images are close-ups of latent palm prints from a burglary investigation. Again, note that the scale is visible and the frame is oriented in order to capture as much detail as possible.

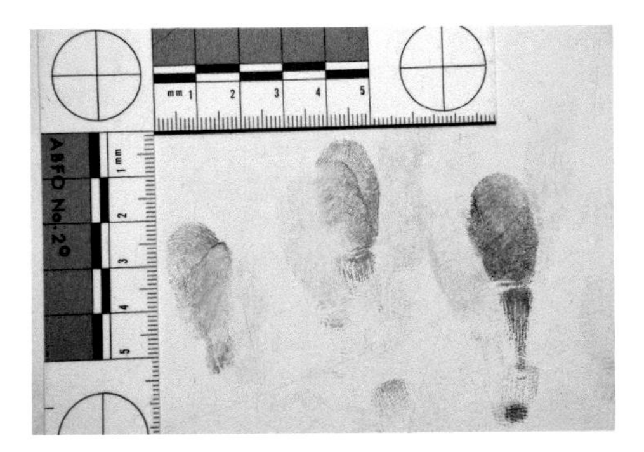

FIGURE 9.3 This represents a close-up of a sequence of three latent prints. After moving from the overall palm, taking a close-up photograph of the digits in sequence, followed by a close-up of the individual digits, is recommended.

危機

CHAPTER 10

Night Photography, Painting with Light, and Long-Shutter Duration Photography

Photographing crime scenes in dark settings can be challenging. This is partially because cameras do not "see" the scene the way our eyes do. Remember our discussion about scenes with a high level of contrast in light? This is referred to as dynamic range. Our eyes have a very large dynamic range, allowing us to see quite well with just a minimal amount of ambient light. Cameras, on the other hand, have a very narrow range in which they can "see" the scene. So, while our eyes tell us that there is enough light to see the scene, the camera will underexpose that same scene unless we take steps to help it capture the image in a way that is usable.

To expose photographs in dark settings, you will have to make efforts to maximize the light and increase the exposure. Since opening the aperture results in a poor depth of field, we recommend that you maintain a middle range, generally f-8 or f-11. The lack of ambient light compounded with a middle range f-stop will thus require the use of a long shutter speed to allow the camera sensor to collect the necessary light for the image. That means we are going to need a tripod. Remember that you will need to stabilize the camera to eliminate the camera shake that is inevitable when we are working with shutter speeds of less than 1/60th of a second.

For certain types of low-light photography, you may be required to use a high ISO. Although we generally recommend avoiding ISOs above 1600, obtaining sufficient light may be very difficult without moving to a higher ISO. In the past, using a high ISO was problematic due to the "noise" created by using a high ISO and a long shutter. More recent cameras have much better performance at high ISOs, so the issue of a noisy image is less of a concern than with older cameras. But we should be aware that high ISO and long duration shutters are going to be "noisier" than using lower ISOs and faster shutter speeds, especially if we are using an older camera. So, while we recommend considering higher ISOs for certain types of low-light photography, we still recommend ISOs below 400 for standard crime scene photography.

Alright, enough of the concepts! Let us get down to the nuts and bolts. You are at a large outdoor scene after dark. You have evidence scattered over a large area, and your flash is just not getting the job done. In the images you have taken, you can see that the flash is reaching out only about 15 feet or so and then the image gets too dark to see anything else. What do you do?

First, place your camera on your tripod. Set the camera to approximately eye level and place it in manual mode. Set your aperture to the aperture needed to get a good depth of field for your camera; f-8 or f-11 will likely yield the best results. Set your ISO to 1600. If a higher setting is available, you can try using it if a lower setting is not achieving the results you need. Using a delayed shutter release or a shutter remote, take a test photo, keeping track of the shutter duration to see where you are with your exposure. Set your focus on manual, as there is usually not going to be enough light to autofocus. Depending on the ambient light levels, you may have enough light to get a good exposure. You will notice that if you have any light sources, light poles, lit signs, etc. in the scene, these will be quite bright. To a certain degree, this is unavoidable. But take a look at your image and see if the light sources in the scene make the image unusable. If so, we will need to add some light to the overall scene to balance out these light sources.

This additional light can be in the form of a flash or a bright floodlight or even a very bright flashlight. Using the same camera settings from our test picture, take another photograph with the addition of the new light source. If using a spotlight or a flashlight, keep the light moving back and forth across the scene in an even manner as if you were painting a wall with it. Also, "paint" the background a bit more than the foreground. The foreground needs less light than the background, so put more light on the background.

Similar results can be achieved with an external flash. The concept is similar to when you are using a flashlight or spotlight, but instead, you will be illuminating the scene with the flash. It is a bit more difficult since the flash is not a steady light source. One technique is to aim the flash into the scene, paying attention to any dark areas and manually activate the flash several times while the shutter is open. Another technique, if you have the workforce and multiple flashes, is to have one person, each with a flash, on each side of the field of view. When the shutter is opened, each person operating a flash will activate the flash, move further down the field of view, and then activate the flash again. This sequence can be repeated as many times as required. This process is an effective method for illuminating very large outdoor scenes at night. We recommend setting your shutter speed to Bulb when performing this painting with light sequence. This will allow you to manually close the shutter instead of the shutter closing at a predetermined time based on the camera settings. You will find that this painting with light sequence may take several minutes.

As mentioned earlier, there are some challenges when painting with light. The first, and most obvious in terms of the image, is that any light source, such as a light pole or lit sign, in the field of view will be very bright and may cause an area of overexposure unless you can balance the light from the light pole with the light from the flashlight or flash. That can be tricky and will usually require several attempts to fine-tune how much painting you have to do with your flashlight or flash. Another challenge to work through is making sure that your foreground and background are evenly lit. Remember that light put into the foreground has a shorter distance to travel to reach the camera, which means it will be brighter than the same amount of light from the background. That means you have to put more light on the background than the foreground. Again, this may take several exposures to get it right.

Here are the step-by-step instructions for both methods.

Painting with Light Using a Flashlight or Other Continuous Light Sources

- Place the camera on a tripod.
- Select f-8 or f-11 for the f-stop.
- Set the ISO to 1600.
- Set the shutter speed to Bulb.
- Manually focus the camera on the scene.
- Using a remote shutter release, press the button allowing the shutter to open.
    - Remember to time the exposure; 15 seconds is a good starting point, in order to make adjustments if the exposure is either over- or underexposed.
- While the shutter is open, paint the scene with the light from your flashlight by panning the light back and forth across the scene.
    - Avoid beginning and ending the stroke in the field of view of the camera, which can cause overexposure in those areas.
    - Remember that it is easy to overexpose the foreground, so favor the background with the center part of the beam, allowing the outer part of the beam to light the foreground.
- Push the remote shutter release and close the shutter.

- Evaluate your exposure and retake the photograph if necessary, adjusting the duration of the exposure to adjust the amount of light.

Painting with Light by Using a Flash: Step by Step

- Place the camera on a tripod.
- Select f-8 or f-11 for the f-stop.
- Set the ISO to 1600.
- Set the shutter speed to Bulb.
- Manually focus the camera on the scene.
- Using a remote shutter release, press the button, allowing the shutter to open.
- While the shutter is open, another person should hold a flash unit over his/her head and aim slightly downward and into the scene. The first flash activation should occur from a position immediately behind the camera.
- The person activating the flash should take about 10 paces, or 30 feet, to the left or right of the camera, then activate the flash again, holding the flash unit in the same manner described above. Be sure to aim the flash straight into the scene, not allowing a left or light deviation. This will help ensure even lighting of the scene.
- After each flash activation, the camera operator should cover the lens with a dark-colored paper or piece of cardboard. This will help ensure even lighting by preventing the collection of light from any other external sources besides the flash. Be sure not to touch the camera or lens during this process, as this will cause a blurry image.

- After each flash activation, the person operating the flash should take about 10 steps forward and then redo the flash activation sequence, each time aiming the flash down and into the scene.
- Perform as many flash activations as necessary to illuminate the scene.
- When the flash activations are completed, depress the shutter to close it.

The technique of painting with light is useful in a variety of different circumstances where you have a large, poorly lit scene. Large, outdoor scenes as you might find on a traffic fatality, or a shooting in a parking lot, lend themselves to this technique. But other types of scenes are also good candidates for using painting with light. The most obvious of these is when doing trajectory analysis with lasers (Figure 10.1) or using a fluorescent blood reagent such as luminol or Bluestar.

The concept is the same, leaving the shutter open long enough to record the laser or the blood reagent while adding enough light to record the entire scene. When using this technique to photograph the light from a laser, the process takes a bit more planning and effort. The camera is placed on a tripod, the laser is turned on, and its light is recorded in the image. That is accomplished by having someone with a large piece of paper, poster board, or similar material walk the path of the laser with the laser projected on to the board. Because the person is moving, and assuming that he/she does not stop, the person is not recorded on the image. The only thing that is recorded is the reflected light from the laser hitting the board. Other available options include the use of specially made smoke available from forensic supply retailers or a fine

FIGURE 10.1 The use of painting with light, even in what are otherwise bright conditions, can be accomplished. In this case, a laser placed on the end of a trajectory rod is used to visualize the trajectory of a fired shot. This photograph was a bit difficult to achieve due to the bright window on the left side of the image. Also complicating things was a large pool of blood in the center of the room, making it difficult to walk the laser across the room.

water mist. You can spray the smoke or water mist into the laser beam, causing it to be visualized and become capable of being photographed. Whatever method you choose, having the scene dark is very helpful. If you are unable to totally darken your scene, it is still possible to obtain a good exposure. After the laser path is recorded, you will use the fill flash technique described in Chapter 3 to briefly illuminate the overall scene. Otherwise, you may end up with only the light from the laser in the image. Also, remember to use manual focus. Trying to use autofocus in a dark room may not work. Because of the complexity of moving through a dark crime scene, and keeping the poster board oriented toward the camera, it is a good idea to have the person walking the poster board practice with the scene lit a few times before taking the photograph.

Here are the step-by-step instructions for laser trajectory photography:

- Set up the laser so that it accurately reflects the trajectory.
- Place the camera on a tripod.
- Select f-8 or f-11 for the f-stop.
- Set the ISO to 1600.
- Set the shutter speed to Bulb.
- Compose the image in the viewfinder by filling the frame and ensuring that both ends of the trajectory are visible.
- Manually focus the camera on the scene.
- Release the shutter, keeping track of its duration.
- While the shutter is open, your assistant will walk along the path of the laser, reflecting the laser using a piece of paper or cardboard, being sure not to stop anywhere along the path of the laser. Alternate methods include the use of smoke or fine water mist.
- Once the assistant has completed the walk along the path of the trajectory, he/she should exit the field of view.
- Using a flash or flashlight, illuminate the scene briefly to allow the overall scene to register on the sensor.
- Release the shutter, allowing it to close.
- Evaluate your exposure and retake the photograph if necessary, adjusting the duration of the exposure or the amount of light added at the end of the exposure, to achieve the proper exposure.

The sequence of photographs in Figure 10.2a through c represents a single gunshot trajectory over a distance of a little over 150 yards. In order to demonstrate that the shot that impacted the occupied residence originated from the suspect's position, a series of three photographs was taken. The first image was taken from inside the backyard. The second image was taken from outside the fence. The third image was taken from a point along the trajectory near the sign, which is common in both of the last two images, to give a sense of continuity between the images. The last image depicts the origin of the shot; a large truck-mounted light source was used to paint the open field where the suspect's body was located. The laser was not moved for the last two photographs (notice that the beam has dispersed considerably). The camera was set up similarly for each photograph. However, in the last two photographs, the person holding the poster board was walking with the poster, in the dark, in an open field, over a distance of more than 100 yards. It was very challenging, but with a few attempts, we were able to get the images we needed.

The settings for this type of photography are going to vary depending on how much light there is in the scene. If it is daylight and you cannot get the room completely dark, you may have to adjust your ISO down and use a smaller aperture to allow the shutter to stay open long enough for this technique. Also, remember that indoors, you are working in a smaller environment, which means you do not need to add much light, like you would for a large, outdoor scene. You will need to set up your camera, record the settings you use, and evaluate the image once it is taken. From there, adjust the settings based on whether you need more or less light. You can try adjusting the

(a)

(b)

FIGURE 10.2 (a–c) This series of images depicts the use of a laser to show the path of a bullet from its origin over 150 yards away. The suspect in this case had fired the shot at the police from an open field, and it impacted the wall of a residence 150 yards away. In order to help corroborate this fact, the trajectory was recorded with the laser in a series of three photographs. For the two images leading from the fence to the open field (a, b), the laser was "walked" along its path by a crime scene investigator running along the trajectory while trying to keep the target aligned with the laser. *(Continued)*

(c)

FIGURE 10.2 (CONTINUED) The area of the open field was painted with light by using a large bank of crime scene lights on a command post vehicle. Without the addition of this light, the image of the laser would have simply disappeared into the night sky. With the light, it can be seen that the laser aligns very closely with where the suspect's body was located (c).

settings, or it may be easier to add or reduce the amount of light you are adding to the exposure. As mentioned in the earlier chapters, practice this technique before you have to use it at a scene. You will quickly develop an eye for what settings you need to use, and your first exposure will more often be close to your intended results. In this photograph, it was important to show where in the doorframe the shot originated. The bright light from the windows was subdued by using a very small aperture. The challenge was not disturbing the blood on the floor.

Photographing blood reagents such as Bluestar or luminol that cause luminescence is similar to laser trajectory photography. Again, some preplanning is necessary. While this technique can be accomplished with one person, it is much easier to do with two people. Because the light from the reagent is usually pretty dim, make the room as dark as possible. You will want to premix your reagent. Place the camera on the tripod, set the aperture to the middle of the range for your camera, and set your ISO to a minimum of 1600. Start with a base setting of 30 seconds for your shutter speed. Using manual focus, focus the camera with lights on and then turn the lights off. Begin applying the reagent to the suspected blood. When you begin to see the luminescence, release the shutter with a delay or a remote shutter release. Continue to apply the reagent to keep the luminescent reaction going. Near the end of the exposure, add a small amount of light to the scene with a flash or a flash-light. This will allow the overall scene to be recorded and still allow the luminescene to be visible. Determining the proper amount of this fill light is going to require practice; each scene is different. The amount of ambient light, intensity of the luminescence, and size of the room are all variables that will change from scene to scene. Figures 10.3 and 10.4 are images of luminescence caused by use of luminol or Bluestar.

Unlike the other techniques discussed in this chapter, you may not get a second chance to take the image due to runoff and dilution of the chemical reagent and blood. This problem may not be encountered on horizontal surfaces, but will surely be an issue on vertical ones. Because of this, we cannot overemphasize how important it is to practice these techniques ahead of time. Without practice, you will be working through the setup of the camera and guessing at how much light to use. With practice, and experience, the process becomes ingrained and much

FIGURE 10.3 This image depicts luminescence after the application of Bluestar. In this instance, a suspect used the sink to wash his hands after murdering his wife.

more second nature. In these examples, one can see how adding the extra light with a flashlight or flash, at the end of the exposure, allows the background to come into view and give the photograph more context in terms of where the footprints were in the garage.

Here are the step-by-step instructions for luminol photography:

- Place the camera on a tripod.
- Select f-8 or f-11 for the f-stop.
- Set the ISO to 1600.
- Set the shutter speed to Bulb of approximately 30 seconds.
- With the scene lit, compose the image in the viewfinder by filling the frame with the area where the luminol will be applied.

(a)

(b)

FIGURE 10.4 These images depict the benefit of adding light to the scene when using luminol or Bluestar to enhance blood in a scene. In (a), the footprints are visible with the Bluestar, but very little else is visible. In (b), the same scene is photographed, but this time, a flashlight was used to add light at the end of the exposure.

- Manually focus the camera on the scene.
- Darken the scene.
- Open the shutter, keeping track of its duration.
- While the shutter is open, have someone apply the reagent to the area and then leave the field of view of the photograph.
- Using a flash or flashlight, illuminate the scene briefly to allow the overall scene to register on the sensor.
- Release the shutter, allowing it to close.
- Evaluate your exposure and retake the photograph if necessary, adjusting the duration of the exposure or the amount of light added at the end of the exposure, to achieve the proper exposure.

危機

CHAPTER 11

Alternate Light Source Photography

Many objects, when illuminated with alternate light sources (ALSs), will fluoresce; that is, they will emit light at higher wavelengths. ALSs are thus commonly employed by crime scene investigators (CSIs) in an attempt to locate evidence that would otherwise be invisible to the naked eye. This latent evidence may fluoresce under varying wavelengths of light, thus enabling visualization so long as specific measures are used to block the wavelength emitted by the ALS. As is the case with any physical evidence, it is important to photograph the evidence in an unaltered condition prior to collection and processing. Unfortunately, one will not be able to capture fluorescence by using standard photography techniques; some specialization is required. Our purpose is not to reiterate existing literature regarding the light spectrum and the physics and chemistry surrounding fluorescence, but to provide simple instructions regarding how to photograph evidence illuminated with an ALS.

To properly photograph evidence fluorescing from an ALS, you will generally require low light conditions. So a tripod and slow shutter speed will be mandatory. In addition, you will be required to use colored barrier filters to block certain wavelengths of light while allowing higher wavelengths to pass through into the camera. Figure 11.1 depicts orange filters, commonly used with light in the blue color spectrum. When purchasing these filters, make sure you order the correct size that fits your lens. You will need to match the lens diameter with the filter diameter. There are some field expedient methods available if you do not have a lens, such as using tinted viewing plates sold through forensic supply distributors, but a lens is much preferred. It is often difficult to block all existing light when using these expedient methods. The passage of even a small amount of certain wavelengths may cause lens flare or other

FIGURE 11.1 Orange filters commonly used with blue light.

problems. So, we would recommend purchasing the required filters and only using these field-expedient methods when absolutely necessary.

Method

- Once evidence is identified with ALS, place the camera on a tripod. Disengage the flash unit.
- Attach the colored barrier filter to the camera lens. The filter should be the same color as the goggles worn by the CSI. The color combination of light and goggles depends on the type of evidence being sought. Most forensic suppliers which distribute ALS units provide guides which dictate light/goggle combinations to use for various items of evidence. The most common crime scene search light is blue, which allows the visualization of a vast array of common evidentiary items. When blue light is used, an orange barrier filter must be used on the camera. This blocks the light emitted by the ALS and allows the visualization of the fluorescence. Other common combinations are green light and red filters and UV light with yellow filters, although often a filter is not required for light in the UV range.

The following chart depicts the preferred light and barrier combinations:

Wavelength (nm)	Light Color	Barrier Color
Less than 470	Violet to blue	Yellow
470–532	Blue to green	Orange
Higher than 532	Green to red	Red

- Focus your lens on the evidence. Depending on the scene, you might use white light to illuminate the evidence or area in order to help you focus.
- Set your camera to aperture priority and your f-stop to f-11. You may also consider using the manual exposure mode, but this will require a bit of shutter speed adjustment after you meter the scene.
- Set the ISO between 400 and 800.
- Illuminate your evidence with the ALS. You might consider panning the evidence evenly; this will prevent bright, overexposed spots.
- Take the photograph. Consider bracketing by using exposure compensation.

Figures 11.2 through 11.5 depict fluorescence emitting from evidence illuminated with blue light

FIGURE 11.2 Bone fragments in gravel illuminated with an ALS unit. A 10-second shutter speed was used to capture this image.

FIGURE 11.3 Fibers in carpet illuminated with an ALS. Higher f-stops were used to improve the depth of field.

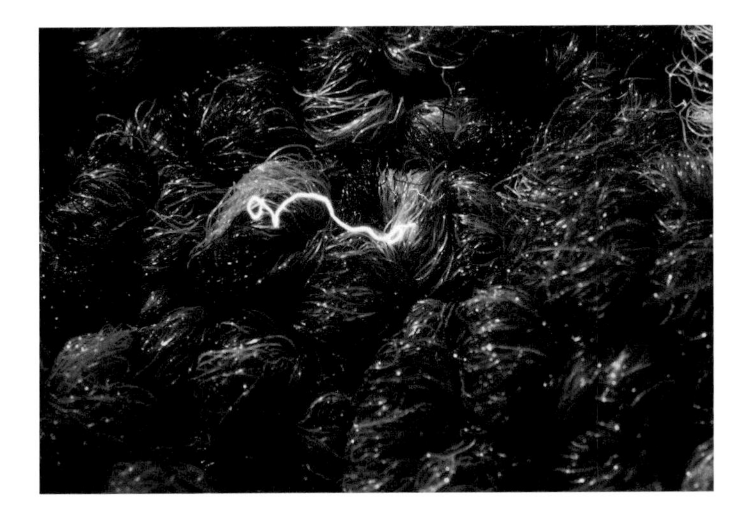

FIGURE 11.4 Another fiber illuminated with ALS.

FIGURE 11.5 Biological fluids and dust particles illuminated with ALS.

(460 nm). An orange barrier filter was used to block the blue light, thus allowing the fluorescence to be visualized.

UV and Infrared

Both UV and infrared wavelengths are sometimes used to locate physical evidence. Both may help visualize bruising. UV may be helpful in locating a wide array of evidence, although caution is advised due to its harmful effects upon deoxyribonucleic acid (DNA). If evidence illuminated with UV is being photographed, you may not require a filter, some UV Light Sources contain violet wavelengths. If this is the case, a yellow filter is required to filter out the violet light, thus allowing the fluorescence to be visualized. Reflected UV light, such as what is used with the Reflected UV Imaging System (RUVIS) which helps to locate latent prints, will require the use of a special filter, called an 18A filter. When using this filter, you may need to adjust your focus.

Infrared light can be used to detect different inks and writing on burned documents and has been reported as being useful in photographing bruises. We have found it especially useful for locating and visualizing gunshot residue on dark surfaces, where it would otherwise go undetected. Most cameras are not equipped to capture infrared light-illuminated evidence. You generally have the choice to remove internal filters from your camera, which we do not recommend unless you possess technical expertise, or purchase a camera specifically designed to capture infrared light. If you have interest in more advanced light source photography techniques, since our focus is on the basics, we recommend Christopher D. Duncan's book, *Advanced Crime Scene Photography*.

危機

Chapter 12

Photographing Vehicles

Photographing a vehicle can be a straightforward process if the crime scene analyst takes the steps necessary to be organized and methodical. Starting with exterior photographs, the vehicle should be photographed from all sides (see Figure 12.1a through h). Any observed damage should be documented with mid-range and close-up photographs if it is part of the investigation, such as a hit-and-run investigation. The license plates, front and rear, if present, should also be specifically photographed. Lastly, the vehicle identification number (VIN) should be photographed. This can be tricky as the windshield is highly reflective and often times dirty. Taking photographs of the location of the VIN before any attempt to clean the area is recommended. In bright light, even with a clean windshield, it can be difficult to overcome the glare. A flashlight shined on the VIN plate, or covering your head and camera with a jacket, can help cut the glare. The use of a polarizer filter will help reduce or even eliminate this glare. Occasionally, you will find that the vehicle dash is dirty and the VIN plate not visible. In this case, you may need to wait until you have accessed the interior of the vehicle and

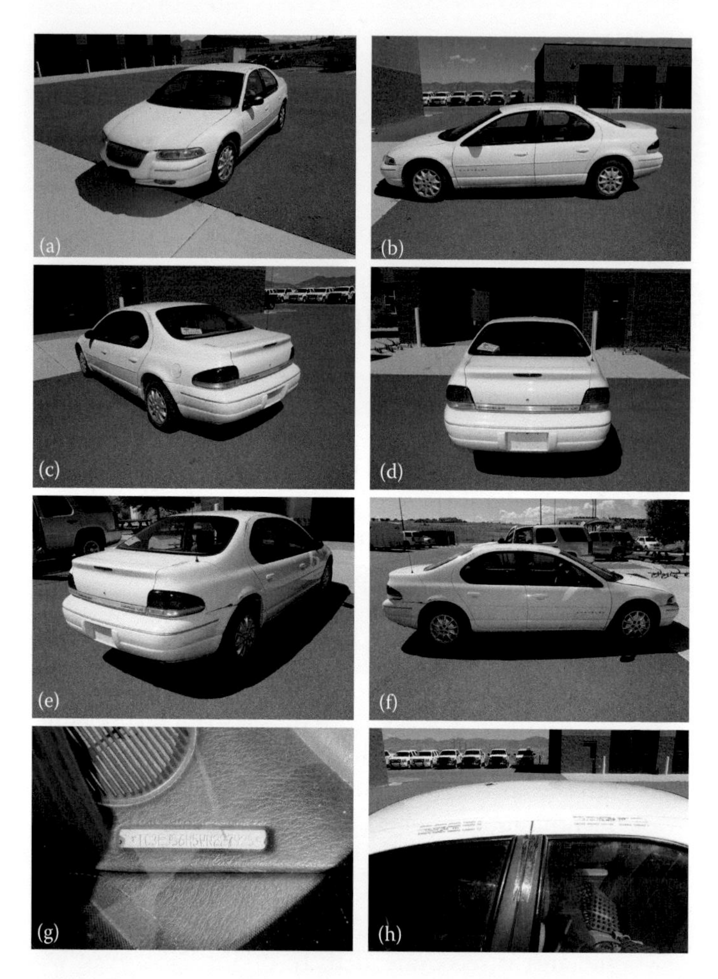

FIGURE 12.1 This series of images shows how to properly sequence the photographs when documenting a vehicle search. After the overall perimeter of the vehicle is photographed, including the door seals, it is best to begin with the front seat, then move around the vehicle, opening doors and photographing the interior as you find it. (a–f) Vehicle exterior; (g) close-up of VIN; (h) image of evidence seals on vehicle. *(Continued)*

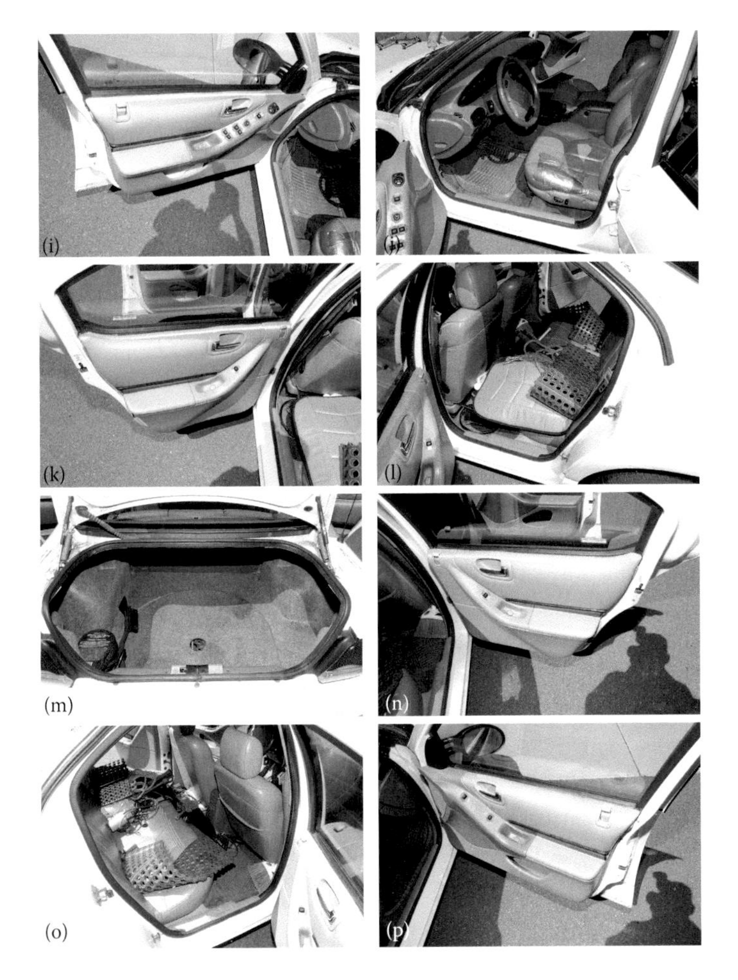

FIGURE 12.1 (CONTINUED) This series of images shows how to properly sequence the photographs when documenting a vehicle search. After the overall perimeter of the vehicle is photographed, including the door seals, it is best to begin with the front seat, then move around the vehicle, opening doors and photographing the interior as you find it. (i) interior of driver's side front door; (j) vehicle interior, front, driver's side perspective; (k) interior of driver's side rear door; (l) vehicle interior, rear compartment, driver's side perspective; (m) trunk compartment; (n) interior of passenger's side rear door; (o) vehicle interior, rear compartment, passenger's side perspective; (p) interior of passenger's side front door. *(Continued)*

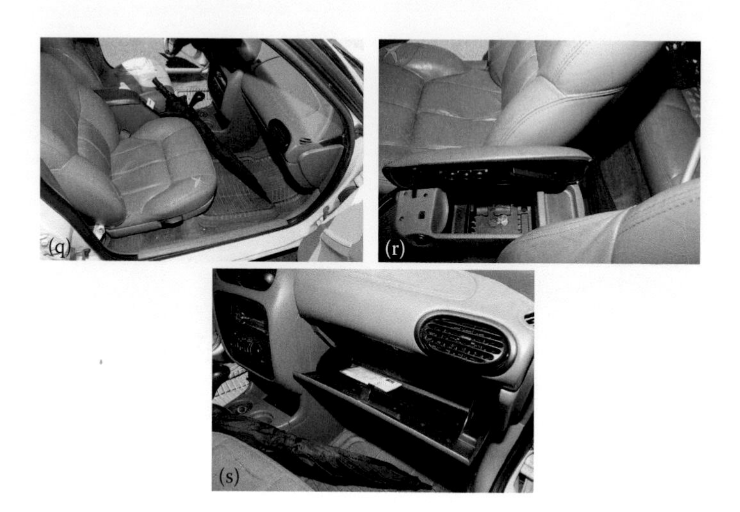

FIGURE 12.1 (CONTINUED) This series of images shows how to properly sequence the photographs when documenting a vehicle search. After the overall perimeter of the vehicle is photographed, including the door seals, it is best to begin with the front seat, then move around the vehicle, opening doors and photographing the interior as you find it. (q) vehicle interior, front, passenger's side perspective; (r) vehicle interior, console area; (s) interior of glove compartment.

photograph the vehicle data decal, usually found on the inner surface of the driver's door.

A couple of things to remember: if photographing a vehicle at night, the use of a flash when photographing the license plates can create a situation where the reflectivity of the license plate will cause the rest of the photograph to be underexposed. In that case, dial down the power of the flash and raise the ISO. This will allow the license plate and the vehicle to be recorded in the photograph. Photographing a vehicle in bright day light can cause deep shadows under the vehicle. Any evidence located in that shadow will likely not be recorded. Fill flash will remedy this problem. Finally, the exterior surface of the vehicle is usually going to be highly reflective. Photographing things like bloodstains in close up will require indirect flash. It is best if the flash is connected via a sync cord and used to create oblique light to avoid washing out the intended area with the reflection.

Once the vehicle exterior has been photographed, it is time to move to the interior (see Figure 12.1i through s). Begin by opening all the doors, trunk, and hood. Then photograph the vehicle around its perimeter once again. Then, choose a section of the vehicle to begin with and photograph the interior of that section. Decide if areas such as a center console are to be considered part of the driver's seat or the passenger seat for purposes of organization. Be sure when photographing a particular section to include areas such as door pockets, glove box, and under the seat. Once one section has been completed, move back out to the exterior of the vehicle and begin the process again, moving from the exterior to the interior to allow easy identification of which area is being photographed. Repeat this process until all sections have been photographed.

You may find that areas such as the back seat or the trunk are cluttered and difficult to photograph in an organized fashion. In this case, work slowly and in layers. Remove a few items at a time, photographing between layers until the seat or bottom of the trunk is reached. When working in this type of situation, it is useful to have a large piece of butcher paper on which to place items. It is recommended that the butcher paper be labeled with the name of the compartment so as to keep track of where an item was found and have the compartment name in the photographs. Placards can also be helpful in keeping the photographs and evidence items organized. If possible, place the placard in the vehicle next to the item of evidence after it has been photographed without the placard. Then, photograph the evidence with the placard, remove the item, and photograph it again with the placard on the butcher paper.

Once all compartments have been photographed, all items that are not being seized as evidence need to be returned to the vehicle. Exit photographs should be taken to document the condition of the vehicle and its contents once all the items have been returned to the vehicle. Lastly, take a photograph of the warrant and the evidence inventory copies that were left in the vehicle.

危機

CHAPTER 13

Injury/Deceased Remains Photography

Photography of injuries and decedents is a vital aspect of the investigative process. Analysis of injuries and conditions of deceased remains may prove critical in understanding the mechanism of injury/death, the characteristics of the weapon involved, and help to answer other questions concerning the time, cause, and manner of death. Obtaining quality images will provide an objective, permanent record of the injuries and conditions of remains. This may be especially important at the scene, since body conditions may change prior to the time of the autopsy.

Photography of deceased remains at a crime scene should occur after the overall photographs are taken, just like other forms of evidence. You will start the sequence with mid-range shots with the goal of depicting the remains in relation to reference points at the scene—again, just as you would with other forms of evidence. Unlike other forms of evidence, however, you will take a series of additional photographs in order to thoroughly capture the characteristics and conditions of the body. The following is the specific sequence we recommend:

- Four photographs of the entire body, one from each side: A wide-angle lens will be very helpful for these photographs since a wide-angle lens will allow a wider perspective. If you are unable to photograph the full body in one image, then take two photographs, one of each half of the body.
- One photograph from directly above the body: To take this photograph, you might find it necessary to affix your camera to a tripod or monopod and hold the tripod/monopod out and over the body. To accomplish the photograph using this method, you would first have to manually focus the camera. You would manually focus on the body from a point equal to the distance that the camera will be from the body, once it is in position over the body. Your camera will need to be precisely configured on the tripod to ensure that the entire body is photographed from an approximately 90° position. Remember that in order to avoid distortion, the 90° angle is important. To help ensure that the entire body is within your photograph boundary, use a wide-angle lens. Once your camera is in position, you will use a remote shutter release to take the photograph. Because you must avoid slow shutter speeds to prevent blur from camera shake, we suggest using flash, specifically manual flash. TTL or automatic flash may result in underexposures. Set your camera to f-22 and the shutter speed to the sync speed (remember that

this will ensure that the shutter closure is coordinated with the flash output to ensure an even, well-exposed photograph).

In lieu of the method described above, you may choose to use a step ladder in order to position yourself in a manner which would allow you to take the image. Be cautious, however, since this could cause scene contamination. You must ensure that the area where the step ladder is placed has already been processed and is void of physical evidence.

- Mid-range photographs of all evidence, injuries, or other significant aspects of the body: These mid-range photographs should be composed in a manner which shows the specific item, or injury, in relation to the individual as a whole. Ideally, if possible, include the face in the photograph. These mid-range photographs will provide context: the viewer can then understand where, on the body, the evidence or injury was located. These mid-range photographs are often overlooked and, in doing so, may create confusion among investigators during later analysis of the images.
- Close-ups of the injuries or evidence without scale: The scale will come later, but the first photograph should depict an unaltered condition. Make sure to fill the frame with the relevant subject matter. This will often require you to position your camera close to the injury or item. A close-up lens will be required.
- Close-ups of injuries or evidence with scale: After the photograph without scale, introduce a scale and take a second photograph. Be very careful—do not allow the scale to touch the

remains. Be mindful that additional photographs will be taken at autopsy, so it is best to skip the scaled photographs if you think you might contaminate the injury or evidence. You may find that forceps will be helpful for holding scales in place for injury photographs.

- After any deceased body is moved, be sure to photograph the side of the body which was previously not visible as well as the area that was underneath the body. We suggest taking these photographs even in the absence of evidence or other noteworthy items. Remember that the absence of evidence may be just as important as its presence, depending on the circumstances of the crime.

Exposure Techniques

You might find it difficult to achieve perfect exposure of bodies using the camera meter as your guide. This is because light-colored skin reflects more light than a normal scene, and conversely, dark-colored skin reflects less light than a normal scene. The result, in both situations, is an overadjustment of the camera's internal metering. So in the case of light skin, your image may often be underexposed since the camera is overcompensating for the light scene. The opposite holds true for dark skin; the camera will overcompensate resulting in an overexposed image.

You may use a couple of approaches to combat the camera's metering problems. First, if you use manual exposure mode, you can adjust your shutter speed or f-stop to compensate for the metering problems. For light skin, you could select a slower shutter speed or a wider aperture to allow more light into the image. Keep in mind the basic rules concerning the selection of shutter speeds and f-stops. Avoid slow shutter speeds (those below the lens length or below 1/60th of a second) if holding your camera, and avoid f-stops below f-8 to ensure a proper depth of field. Secondly, you may use aperture or shutter priority exposure modes and adjust exposure through the exposure compensation function. Simply add light for light skin and reduce light for dark skin. Figure 13.1 depicts bite marks that were photographed using different exposure settings.

Keep in mind that the use of flash will negate exposure problems, but the downside is that flash will often cause glare or hotspots on bodies. You can consider the use of bounce flash or other flash diffusion methods described in Chapter 3, but we often find it easier to avoid flash altogether. In dimly lit scenes, this might require the use of a slow shutter speed and, thus, a tripod, but the results may well be worth the extra effort.

FIGURE 13.1 These are images of a bite mark on skin. Different exposures were used to help visualize the individual impressions. Notice that an L-scale was used, which is preferred for bite mark photography.

Injury Photographs on Living Persons

The process for photographing injuries on live persons consists of identification photographs(s), mid-range shots which establish the location of the injury on the body, and a series of close-ups. The first photograph should include the face of the person, serving as an identification shot. After the identification photograph, mid-range photographs should be taken to reveal the location of the injury in relation to the body as a whole. Finally, close-ups should be taken of the actual injury, first without a scale, and then with a scale. Figure 13.1 depicts close-ups of a bite mark injury. We recommend using an L-shaped scale for this purpose. It will be important to keep the scale on the same plane as the evidence.

Although the general procedure for photographing injuries on living persons is quite similar to photographing deceased remains, there are some distinctions that require a specialized approach. First, generally speaking, you must obtain permission to take the photographs. Usually, this requires the consent of the person being photographed. Secondly, you must account for the fact that the person can move. Asking them to stay still may work, but if you are photographing a young child, this may prove challenging! With some patience, you should be able to achieve your goal; although an alternative might be to use a faster shutter speed to account for some movement. Finally, since injuries sometimes become more visible as time passes, you should consider photographing injuries at intervals over the next few days. Remember that an alternate light source may also help detect injuries that may not be visible to the naked eye.

You may also encounter injuries in the genital or other sensitive areas of the body. Of course, it is always wise to follow formal department procedures when photographing sensitive areas. Many departments may require the photographer to be the same gender as the person being photographed. We also recommend taking the photographs in a manner which can reduce embarrassment to the person. For example, if you are photographing an injury of a sexual assault victim's inner thigh, you can crop the image to exclude external genitalia. You may also consider the use of a sheet or other object to cover the sensitive areas. Of course, if external genitalia are injured, you will have to photograph the injuries. These photographs may be inherently embarrassing, but the goal is to ensure that the photograph appears professional and does not present the victim in a manner which could prejudice a jury.

Autopsy Photography

Many investigators, depending on jurisdiction, are assigned to photograph autopsies. Some of the main objectives of a forensic autopsy are to document the condition of the decedent and recover physical evidence. Naturally, photography is a critical component of this documentation process. You will follow the same guidelines as you would when photographing a crime scene. Your photographs should be properly exposed and have a sufficient depth of field. Modern autopsy suites are very well lit; thus, exposure may not be extremely burdensome. That being said, you may still choose to use flash. Using flash will help ensure even lighting, fill in shaded areas, and help account for light and dark skin exposure issues. Also, it will help you maximize the depth of field since you will be able to use a relatively fast shutter speed. Maximizing the depth of field is critical in autopsy photography, especially when photographing injuries with depth. Remember that to maximize the depth of field, you should avoid low number f-stops.

The initial portion of a forensic autopsy consists of an external examination of the body, starting with a description of clothing; appearance; and any visible marks or injuries, scars, or tattoos. To properly photograph the external examination, you should take one photograph of the entire body from all four sides, just as you would at a crime scene. Since the autopsy suite is a controlled environment, you should find this process easier to complete since fewer obstructions will be present. You should also take one photograph of the entire body from directly overhead. We recommend the use of a step ladder to help in this process. The next photograph will be an identification photograph. In this identification shot, you will fill the frame with the decedent's face and head. For this photograph, make sure that your camera body is parallel to the decedent's face and use a lens length between 100 and 120 mm to avoid distortion. Once the medical examiner or autopsy technician turns the body over, you will then photograph the side of the body that was previously not visible.

The next step in the process is to take a series of mid-range and close-up photographs of anything significant found on or in the body or clothing. Examples may include scars, injuries, emergency medical intervention materials, and so on. Any mid-range photograph should establish the location of the significant item in relation to the body as a whole.

Close-ups should fill the frame. Remember to take close-ups first without a scale, then with a scale.

After clothing is removed, photographs of the body should be taken again in the same manner as the first series (from all sides and above). Again, you should take mid-range and close-up photographs of any significant items.

All subsequent steps of the autopsy, including the internal examination, recovery of evidence, and tissue/fluid withdrawal, should be photographically documented. Although it may be difficult for the investigator to determine the significance of some internal findings, the medical examiner should draw your attention to anything that may be relevant to the investigation. The medical examiner will examine all organs and various tissues, depending on the case. We recommend photographing each step of this process.

The following is a step-by-step summary of autopsy photography steps (Figure 13.2):

- Start by taking photographs of the entire body from all four sides, then from directly overhead.
- Take a photograph of the decedent's face and head, from a 90° angle to the face, to serve as an identification photograph. Use a 100–120 mm lens.
- Take mid-range and close-ups (without and with scale) of any significant items, such as injuries, scars, and tattoos.
- Repeat this process after clothing is removed.
- After the external examination is complete, photograph each portion of the internal examination. Take mid-range photographs and close-ups of any significant items or findings. During

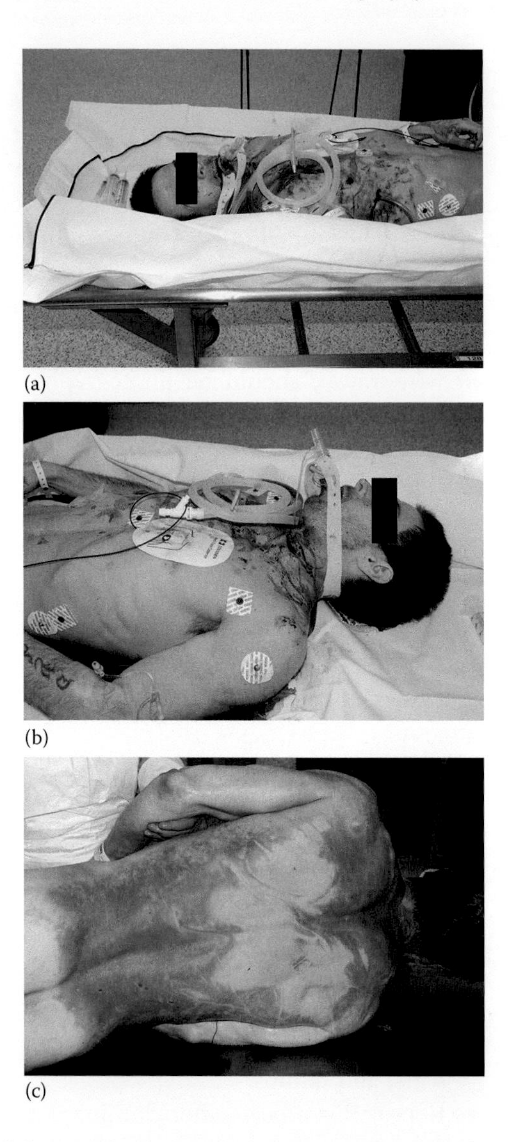

FIGURE 13.2 Included are some of the required autopsy images showing the external condition of the body and several significant injuries present on the decedent. (a) One of the initial images taken after sheet was removed from the body; (b) overall image of the victim's upper torso; (c) overall image of the upper torso of the body (notice the livor mortis). *(Continued)*

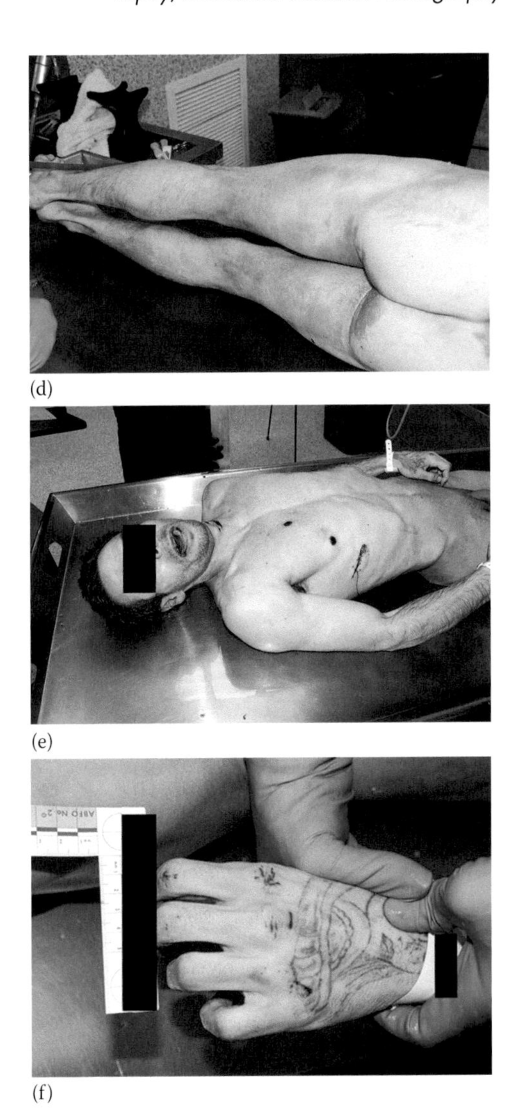

FIGURE 13.2 (CONTINUED) Included are some of the required autopsy images showing the external condition of the body and several significant injuries present on the decedent. (d) overall image of the victim's lower torso; (e) victim's upper torso and face (it helps to establish the location of some of the victim's injuries); (f) injuries to the victim's hands (these types of injuries are consistent with defense wounds). *(Continued)*

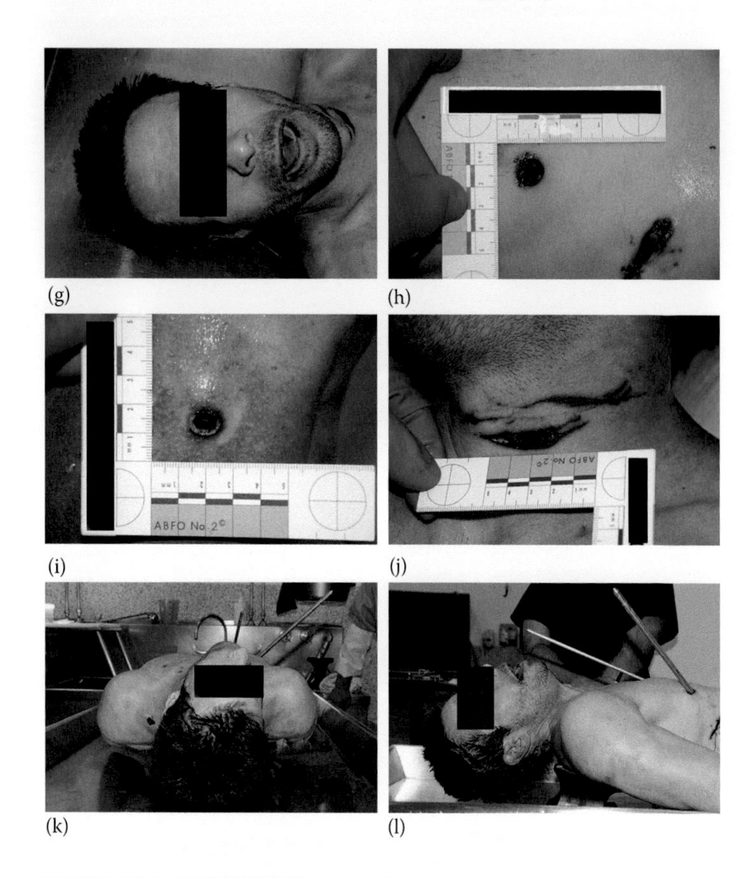

FIGURE 13.2 (CONTINUED) Included are some of the required autopsy images showing the external condition of the body and several significant injuries present on the decedent. (g) identification image; (h, i) close-ups of a gunshot wound; (j) close-up of a sharp force injury; (k) trajectory rods used by the medical examiner to display the bullet pathway through the body; (l) trajectory rods from a different perspective (using a variety of perspectives is often very useful).

the internal examination portion of the autopsy, the medical examiner staff should draw your attention to significant items since some of these may not be readily apparent if you are not specially trained in forensic pathology.

- Any physical evidence discovered (such as a projectile) should be photographed in place before removal. Once the evidence is removed from the body, you may consider taking additional close-up photographs if warranted. An example would be to photograph portions of the object which could not be seen while in the body.
- While it is considered best practice to eliminate backgrounds that include medical equipment, other investigators, etc., it may not be possible in every situation. Large autopsy suites with multiple autopsies taking place simultaneously may make eliminating the background a practical impossibility. As best you can, drape the background to reduce distractions. But remember that unless you are employed by the medical examiner's office, you are a guest. Do not insist on draping the background if it interferes with the examination by the medical examiner.

Figure 13.2 includes some of the images that should be taken at a forensic autopsy.

Index

Page numbers followed by f and t indicate figures and tables, respectively.

F

G

H

I

L

R

S

T